MY JERUSALEM ENCOUNTER

Geoffrey Cohen

Original Print Version
Copyright © 2013 by Geoff Cohen
Published by Gateway Create Publishing

Visit geoffreycohen.com for additional ministry information.

www.BurkhartBooks.com

Bedford, Texas

Dedication

I dedicate this book to the God of Abraham, Isaac, and Jacob, the God of my fathers, who keeps his covenant and always remains faithful to me and to my people, from generation to generation, despite our hearts that tend to wander from his ways.

I also dedicate this book to those who seek him with all their hearts, for they will find him.

Endorsements

"In *My Jerusalem Encounter*, Geoff Cohen has provided us with a very interesting and very human story, describing his experience as a man making a journey of faith; one that will inspire many and bewilder some. I urge Jews and Christians alike to read it. Geoff has touched the nerve of a contemporary phenomenon described as Messianic Judaism—a faith that respects both traditions and blends them, without compromising the ethnicity of a wholehearted Jew nor the authenticity of a biblically defined Christian. This is a man who has met the Living God and found that His love and truth are not in conflict. When the Old and New Testaments are examined, we discover that both of these historic traditions welcome love's truth, and truth's fullness."

Jack W. Hayford,
Chancellor at The King's University
Los Angeles, CA

"I first heard Geoff"s story as we walked the streets of Jerusalem together, and I remember saying "What?" "Wow!" and "Incredible!" about a hundred times as he told me how the Lord revealed Himself to him in such a powerful manner. Geoff Cohen's story is one of the most inspiring I have ever heard. His story had to be told. As you read it you won't just be inspired by what you read about this journey - you will find renewed hope and courage for the challenges you are facing."

Jimmy Evans
Author/Senior Elder of Trinity Fellowship Church/Founder of Marriage Today
Amarillo, TX

"*My Jerusalem Encounter* gives the reader life-changing insight into the faithfulness of God in every situation. I can't imagine a more heart-stirring account of the life of a Jewish man discovering Yeshua as his Messiah. Geoffrey is so transparent as he tells his story, and the triumphant feel the reader finds within the pages of this book will increase one's awe of a mighty God."

Olen Griffing
Founding Pastor of Shady Grove Church
Grand Prairie, TX

"Geoffrey Cohen is an incredible Jewish believer with an amazing testimony. His book will encourage you and help you to understand the unique challenges faced by Jews who have come to embrace Jesus as their Messiah."

Jonathan Bernis
President and CEO Jewish Voice Ministries, International
Phoenix, AZ

"A South African Jew growing up during the apartheid years, who finds his way to America via Jerusalem, makes for an intriguing and compelling story. Geoff paints his personal story with a full palette of color. I was drawn in completely. I highly recommend this modern day story of Jewish redemption."

Wayne Hilsden
Senior Pastor King of Kings Assembly
Jerusalem, Israel

"Geoffrey Cohen's story and testimony is both riveting and life changing for those who hear it or read it. It is the story of one man's relentless pursuit of Israel's promised Messiah, which culminates in a dramatic encounter between the two. I highly recommend this book for anyone who is trying to discover who God really is."

Chris Hodges
Senior Pastor of Church of the Highlands/ Author of *Fresh Air*
Birmingham, AL

Table of Contents

Acknowledgments

So many people have played such an important role in my life that I won't be able to acknowledge them all.

First, I want to thank God, without whom I would not have a story to tell.

I want to thank my incredible and beautiful wife, Tatiana, through whom I have found true love, life and a new beginning. She challenges me and inspires me every day to reach to new heights in God and as a person. I love her with all my heart.

I want to thank my parents, Ronald Sydney Cohen and Zena Cohen, for being the best parents they could be through some tough trials, especially having been raised in a country that was in such great turmoil. I want to specifically thank my mom for patiently giving me many invaluable details about our family history that have added so much depth to this book.

I want to thank Allen Shoulders for believing in me and in my calling, and for encouraging me to write this book and to be bolder about pursuing my destiny.

Last, I want to thank every person who has ever believed in me and encouraged me, including my friends Craig Beling, Manfred and Isit Nochomowitz, Ronny and Laura Wilson and so many others who I do not have the space to mention.

Foreword

Sometimes, great destinies are built out of misfortune.

Such is the story of Geoffrey Cohen, Gateway Church's Pastor of Jewish Ministries, and a friend of mine. As you'll read in *My Jerusalem Encounter*, God used what appeared to be many difficulties to draw Geoffrey to Him, and eventually set him on the path to becoming one of the world's most influential Messianic ministers.

That path eventually led Geoffrey and his family to Gateway Church, where he has served since 2006. Under his leadership, our Messianic Service—the first service Gateway Church holds each month—has grown to be one of the largest of its kind in the U.S. That's because Geoffrey Cohen has a strong call on his life to reach the Jewish people. And, because he is a man who truly understands the importance of following God's order for world evangelism, he has traveled the world preaching the gospel where he has seen the hearts of countless Jews and Gentiles alike turned to Jesus.

As you'll read in this book, Geoffrey grew up in a South African Jewish community. Throughout his formative years he struggled in vain to find his identity as a Jew. Finally, a face-to-face encounter with Jesus truly changed everything.

I've been saved for over thirty years now. Not only did I change drastically after I first met Jesus, but I've continued to grow as my revelation of Him grows. The Bible is filled with stories of people who had similar experiences. Perhaps the most famous example is Saul, the persecutor of Christians, who became the Apostle Paul after he met Jesus on the road to Damascus. One of my favorite examples is the Apostle John, whom Jesus called a "Son of Thunder." John actually asked Jesus for permission one time to call down fire from heaven upon people (Luke 9)! This is the same man who years later wrote the words, "Love one another, for love comes from God" (1 John 4:7).

That sounds like a completely different person! What changed him? Continual encounters with Jesus.

I know everything changed for Geoffrey after his "Jerusalem encounter," but it didn't stop there. He has dedicated his life to helping others receive the same revelation of Jesus as the Messiah that he received all those years ago.

When you encounter Jesus, your life will change. Geoffrey is a living example of this, and I can't imagine anyone better to encourage you on your own journey of meeting and walking with Jesus. It is my hope that *My Jerusalem Encounter* will not only inspire you, but that it will draw you closer to Jesus the Messiah, just as it did for Geoffrey Cohen.

Robert Morris
Senior Pastor of Gateway Church
Southlake, TX

Introduction

I am an ordinary guy who had an extraordinary experience with God.

I spent decades searching for God and for meaning in life. My quest took me to three continents, from Africa to the Middle East to North America, and I interacted with people from every spectrum of life. My journey culminated with a supernatural encounter in Jerusalem that changed my life forever. To my surprise, I found out that God had been searching for me even harder than I was searching for him. He hadn't been hiding at all, merely waiting for me to respond to his quest for me.

I first shared my story in the summer of 1984. Since then I have told it in twenty-two nations, on radio and television around the world, in churches, Bible schools, and messianic synagogues, one on one, in prisons, at retirement homes, and even in militant Muslim nations. Wherever I have presented my story, people's lives have been impacted and many have changed for eternity as a result.

For almost twenty-eight years, people have been asking me to write a book about my life. You may wonder why it took so long for me to tell this story. But God has perfect timing, and his timing for you to read this is now.

God is searching for you, calling to you in the deep alleyways and recesses of your heart. He is reaching out to you in the hope that you will respond to him in love. He promises, "You will seek me and find me when you seek me with all your heart" (Jeremiah 29:13 NIV).

This is my story, but it can be your story too. I invite you to enter into this journey of life with me. I pray that as you read these pages, you will embark on your own adventure of a lifetime.

Prologue

In the early 1900s, orthodox priests in Russian-dominated Eastern Europe accused the Jews of deicide for killing Christ. They preached fiery sermons against the Jews, especially during Easter, painting them in a demonic light. Rumors were spread that Jews were killing Christian children and using their blood to make matzo for Passover.

As ridiculous as these lies were, people who attended the local Catholic and Russian Orthodox churches believed them. They started invading Jewish villages, called *shtetls*, where Jews lived together in cohesive, self-sustaining communities in order to maintain their culture, religion, language, and traditions. These attacks usually had an orthodox priest at the helm, carrying a huge cross as if he were on a mission from God. Russian Cossacks on horses led these violent pogroms and encouraged local Christian peasants to join in. They raped, maimed, and killed innocent Jews and destroyed Jewish shops and properties, believing they were doing God a service by getting revenge on the Jews for supposedly murdering his Son.

These people were never prosecuted. The government turned a blind eye, happy to use the Jews as a scapegoat for Tsar Nicholas II's failing regime.

My mother's father, Leslie Herring, grew up in one such Jewish shtetl in Lithuania called Panevzys. When he was about eight years old, his village was attacked around Easter time. When he heard the thundering of horses' hooves, and saw helpless older men and women being beaten with the backs of rifles and trampled underfoot, he ran for his life and hid in a haystack in a barn. Moments later, laughing soldiers stabbed through the hay with bayonets. A few of the spikes narrowly missed Leslie's head. He stifled screams, terrified of moving a muscle or making a sound. After what seemed like an eternity, they gave up the search and left.

Leslie's father, Isaac, was a huge man—about six foot six, with large hands and feet—and very strong. His wife, Nachama, was quite small—about five feet tall, with hands and feet that seemed tiny in comparison. They made for an odd-looking couple.

A Russian army base in their village recruited young men from Jewish families who had more than one son. The oldest sons of all Jewish families were forced to serve in the czar's army if they were twenty-one or older.

Since Isaac had a younger brother, he was recruited for the Russian military. His great size and powerful strength made him a prime choice. Unfortunately, because of the harsh winter conditions, he contracted a respiratory condition that attacked his lungs and resulted in a terrible persistent cough.

There was no cure for Isaac's condition, but the doctor told him he could prolong his life if he moved to a higher altitude, where the air was thinner. He mentioned there was a gold rush in South Africa, and a good living could be made there if he opened a convenience store serving the miners. There was an especially great need in Krugersdorp, just outside Johannesburg, which had an altitude of about six thousand feet above sea level. Many Jewish Lithuanians had emigrated there, and it seemed to offer a safe haven for them.

So Isaac decided to move to South Africa. His wife would stay behind to fend for their two young daughters (Fanny and Betty) and two sons (my grandfather Leslie and his brother, Phillip). When he had found a home, Isaac would bring the rest of the family over by ship.

He set up shop and began to do very well in a short span of time. Unfortunately, soon after he arrived in South Africa, World War I broke out, so the plan for his family to join him failed. His wife was left alone, stuck with the responsibility of raising four kids on her own through severe winters in the middle of the biggest war the world had ever known.

With no marketable skills, Nachama became a bootlegger. As a young boy, Leslie helped support the family by grooming the Russian soldiers' horses for half a loaf of black bread per day. (He developed a great love for horses, and as an adult he bred them. One of them ended up winning best-in-show.)

Being a single mother in such harsh times made Nachama and her children extremely vulnerable. Russian soldiers could do whatever they wanted when they came to a Jewish village, and they were known for brutality and raping.

One day, a couple of soldiers found Nachama alone with her two young daughters. They grabbed the helpless, screaming girls. Nachama's strong protective instincts overcame her diminutive size. As the soldiers were about to rape her children, she grabbed a large garden spade and hit them on the backs of their heads with all her strength. She continued beating them until they were both dead. She then buried the bodies so the Russian army would never find out. Those soldiers paid the ultimate price for messing with a Jewish mama's daughters!

After WWI ended, Nachama, my grandfather Leslie (who was then twelve), his brother Phillip, and their two sisters boarded a ship headed for South Africa. When they arrived, Isaac was waiting to greet them, eager to see his family. Leslie had been so young when he left home, his father looked like a stranger to him.

In 1936, Leslie was introduced to a young woman in her twenties who had just moved to South Africa from her Jewish village in Lithuania. Fruma's brothers had come out earlier, but she'd stayed behind to care for their ailing mother. After the mother died, Fruma joined her brothers.

The two families knew each other, as they had lived in neighboring villages in Lithuania. Nachama told Leslie that when Fruma was just a few months old, she had taken her children to visit the family. Fruma's mom took one look at handsome four-year-old Leslie, grasped his little hand, and told him in strong Yiddish, *"Kumen un visn dayne*

Kale," which means "Come and meet your bride." Of course, he had no clue what she was talking about at the time.

After being separated for more than two decades by two wars and thousands of miles, they met in South Africa. It was love at first sight and they married shortly thereafter. Fruma's mother's "prophecy" had been fulfilled.

In 1941, the Nazis advanced toward Russia through Lithuania. They sent SS troops ahead of the army, who annihilated entire Jewish villages, including Kupiskis, where Fruma had been born and raised. Nazis took all the citizens at gunpoint to a nearby forest and made them dig huge holes that were meant to serve as their graves. After forcing them to strip naked, the soldiers gunned down men, women, and children with machine guns.

Out of almost 1,500 Jews in the village of about three thousand people, only one rabbi survived to tell the story. He was shot in the arm but managed to escape into the woods.

On August 25, 1941, German soldiers and Lithuanian conspirators attacked Panevyzs—the village Leslie was born and raised in, which was just a few miles away from Kupiskis. They herded 150 Jewish families like cattle and crammed them into a building in the central marketplace, which was then set on fire. They were burned alive, to the musical accompaniment of a German military band. The rest of the Jewish inhabitants were taken to the forests surrounding the village and gunned down by the Nazis and their Lithuanian conspirators.

Both of the villages where Fruma and Leslie were raised had been more than half Jewish before the war. Afterward, there was not one Jew left. When the Nazis succeeded in their devilish mission, they declared those areas *Judenrein,* or "free from Jews."

If my great-grandfather Isaac did not have the respiratory disease that made him seek out a land with a higher altitude so he could live a longer life, he and his family would have been wiped out with the rest of the people in his village.

If my grandmother Fruma had not left her village in Lithuania to join her brothers after their mother died, she would have been murdered by the Nazis who attacked her village a few years later.

This series of seemingly random, disconnected events and decisions turned out to be divine providence. My family, who had lived in Eastern Europe for centuries, was saved by being moved out of harm's way before the Holocaust extended its deadly tentacles to us.

This is how I came to be born in South Africa, which is where my story begins.

1

DURBAN, MY CHILDHOOD PARADISE

I stood outside the store, loading chocolate bars into the leather bag on the back of my bike, and looked down on my home. From the top of this hill, I could see all of Westville, a budding suburb of Durban in South Africa. Our yard, with its huge trees, great for climbing and building tree houses, sat in the midst of acres upon acres of tall elephant grass, which was tremendous fun to hide and play in. Furry gray vervet monkeys scampered in the trees, with their cute black faces and tiny hands.

"If you don't hurry up, we won't make it home before sundown." My nine-year-old sister, Barbara, already seated on her girly bike, gave me a concerned look. Being the older sibling, and a female, she was like a second mother to me whenever our mom wasn't around. She'd even protected me from bullies in kindergarten.

"No problem, Barbs," I said, hopping onto my British-made BSA. "I'm the fastest cyclist around. I bet I could go even faster than a car." At seven years old, I felt confident about my abilities. And while Barbara was always slow and cautious, I was wild and loved speed.

I eyed the steep, half-mile road that led directly to our house. The hill ended at a stop sign. After the intersection was a sudden drop flanked by two huge grassy banks, then the six-foot-high concrete fence that surrounded our property.

"Don't go too fast, Geoff. Mom and Dad will be angry if you wreck that bike." Barbie was always cautious. I didn't see any point in ever going slow.

Eager to leave my sister far behind, and hoping to break the world downhill land speed record for a seven-year-old, I pedaled as hard as my little legs could. Faster and faster I flew. Everything around me blurred. The wind rushed past my cheeks and whipped my hair every which way.

In an instant, the pedals came loose, turning faster than ever but without any traction. The chain had come off! Since the bike had pedal brakes, that meant I had no way to stop.

I quickly weighed my options. If I turned left, I'd run into a wire fence. Turning right would send me crashing into a huge tree. Seeing no way out, I locked my elbows, gripped the handlebars, and went straight ahead.

I shot past the stop sign, thanking God there were no cars to crash into at that moment. My relief was short-lived.

When I reached the drop with the two grassy banks, I was going so fast that my bike went airborne. For a brief moment, I soared through the air as if I were flying. Unfortunately, I was headed straight for our concrete fence. I gripped the handlebars and straightened my elbows, bracing for the inevitable impact.

My front tire slammed into the top of the fence. I vaulted over the handlebars and slid down the rough concrete. I landed facedown in the sandy soil of our flowerbed. As I lay there, tears streaming down my face, I fully expected to be taken straight into heaven that very moment.

When I realized I'd survived the crash, with no injuries at all apart from a scrape on my right cheek, I laughed. Once again, the hand of God had spared me. Miraculously, the thick front tire and strong frame of the BSA bike had absorbed most of the impact.

I recalled the numerous other close calls I'd had in my short life and how the invisible hand of God had rescued me every time.

One of my earliest memories was of Rosie, our loving and faithful Zulu housemaid, bathing me with a sponge. As I stood in the bath, I slipped and fell and cut my eye. With blood gushing down my face, she carried me to my room and I was rushed to the hospital. The cut was deep, but it missed the eye.

At five years old, I was playing with my plastic train on the porch when a long green snake slithered on the grass toward me. "Look," I cried out. "It's a *shongolulu*!" I ran to go play with it.

At that moment my mom came outside. When she saw what was happening, she screamed, "Geoffrey, come back immediately!"

She only called me Geoffrey when she was either angry or serious. And I could tell by the tone in her voice that this was urgent. So I hurried back to the porch. My mom called Rosie, who came out with a pitchfork and drove it through the creature's head.

"Why'd she do that?" I asked, trembling.

"That was a green mamba," she explained, "one of the most poisonous snakes on the planet. Its venom could have killed you in twenty minutes or less."

I knew it was a miracle that I hadn't been bitten.

Shortly after my seventh birthday, I was playing at the beach with my cousins who were visiting from Canada during the summer. Since we had a pool at our house, and I swam in it as often as I could, I was a strong swimmer for my age. Because it was low tide, I went out into the deep water.

Suddenly, the ground beneath me disappeared, as if I'd been

standing on the back of a whale. The strong current of the mighty Indian Ocean pulled me out to sea. Waves crashed over my head. To my left, huge rocks dwarfed me. In front of me were buoys that held up large underwater nets. The waters beyond those nets were infested with sharks.

My little arms and legs grew tired of keeping me afloat as waves continued crashing over my head. How much longer could I last?

Suddenly, a strong arm wrapped around my neck and pulled me back to shore. As my rescuer swam with my head locked in a lifesaver's grip, I swallowed a lot of water. Eventually, he got me onto the shore. He placed me on my towel, face down, and I repeatedly coughed up water. When I could breathe, I sobbed uncontrollably, relieved to be safe and on dry land, glad to be alive and with my family again.

If one of my cousins hadn't spotted me and alerted the lifeguard, I would have drowned.

Over and over, my life had been spared. Even at this young age, I knew God had a plan for me.

As I lay on the grass beside the concrete wall around our property, I wondered what lay in store for my future. But at that moment, the biggest thing on my mind was how I could explain at school how after such a severe accident I only ended up with a scrape on my cheek!

———◆———

As I hobbled across the lawn toward the house with my bicycle, Rosie came running out to me, her long, colorful dress billowing behind her. Barbara must have told her about my latest near-death experience.

Tears streaming down her dark cheeks, Rosie wrapped her hefty arms around me and lifted me off the ground, enveloping me in one of her familiar, comforting embraces. Leaving the bike behind, she half-carried me to the bathroom, where she helped me change into clean clothes, washed the dirt off of me, and gently dabbed my scuffed-up knees and elbows with soothing medicine.

I loved our Zulu maid. From the time I was an infant, Rosie had nurtured me even more than my mother. Mom was a wonderful, kind woman, but she and Dad were very social and went out a lot, leaving me and Barbie in Rosie's capable and loving care. When I was a baby, she carried me on her back in a big, soft blanket—in traditional Zulu fashion—and rocked me to sleep with a soothing native lullaby. "*Tula too, tula baba, tula sana,*" she sang, meaning "Stop crying, little baby, stop crying." Her melodic voice soothed me until I drifted off into a peaceful sleep.

Because of Rosie, I had a special fondness for Zulus. I loved all the eleven major tribes in South Africa, but none struck fear in the hearts of their enemies like the Zulu nation did. They were a proud, strong people descended from the legendary kings Chaka and Dingaan. They had a fighting spirit that I admired, and their bravery and loyalty made them seem like invincible heroes to my mind.

To my amazement, my bike didn't have a single dent or scratch on it. After I put it in the garage, I joined my family in the dining room—barely in time for the beginning of our Sabbath meal.

As the man of the house, my father sat at the head of the table, which was draped in a white linen tablecloth. I took my seat to his right, as the "man" of my future household. Barbara, seated across from me, raised an eyebrow at me, but she didn't say a word about my crazy stunt.

My grandfather sat at the foot of the table, with Grandmother next to him on my side. Mom and Tracy were next to Barbara. I winked at my three-year-old sister. Trace was as cute as could be with her mop of curly brown hair.

When I was four years old and Mom announced she was pregnant, I was convinced I'd have a brother. I wanted someone I could wrestle and do other boyish things with. On March 7, 1966, when my parents got a curly-haired baby girl, I went around proclaiming that I had a new brother and his name was Alan! But Tracy turned out to be something of a tomboy, and we had lots of fun together. I could do almost anything with her that I could do with a brother, except wrestle.

Mom stood, and we all joined her to usher in the Sabbath. She lifted the white linen cloth covering the braided challah. I breathed in the heavenly scent of this delicious white bread, which was shiny from being coated in egg whites prior to baking, giving it a "varnished" look.

My mother said the Hebrew blessing over the bread and lit the candles in their sterling silver holders. Then Dad recited the traditional Sabbath prayers from the Hebrew Siddur, holding the prayer book as reverently as if it contained a fortune in gold rather than liturgies for ceremonial Jewish observances. I knew the prayers by heart and joined in with my father as the only other "man" in the home except for my grandfather, who said the Sabbath prayers when we were at his house.

By the time we sat down to eat, an almost tangible peace had descended over our home. I loved this Friday-evening tradition that focused on God and family.

After the meal, we all gathered in the living room, where the adults chatted and we kids played with toy trains, cars, dominoes, and the family dogs.

Around 9:30, my grandparents left for home so they could get a good night's sleep before going to synagogue the next day. My family occasionally attended services on Saturday, but most of the time we spent the day together, resting after the busy week.

I spent all day Saturday outdoors, swimming, riding my bike, climbing trees, and racing my go-kart down the hill with our neighbors.

I loved the thrill of riding that little wooden vehicle, which I'd made myself using wheels from an old lawn mower and a crude piece of wood that touched the tires when I needed to brake.

On Sunday morning, I swam in our backyard pool, waiting for my best friend, Gordon Fletcher, to get home from church. Most of our neighbors were Jewish, as were all of my school friends. Gordon was the only non-Jewish boy I knew. And he lived right next door.

Gordon's parents were Scottish, and his older brother played the bagpipes. They loved the queen and celebrated Christmas and Easter. Apparently that was what Christians did.

Though I found their Christian home quite strict, I liked the atmosphere there. I knew the Fletchers had different religious beliefs from ours, but I didn't care. He was my friend, and that was all that mattered to me.

After Gordon changed out of his church clothes and into a swimsuit, he bolted out of his front door and joined me at the pool. We tied towels around our necks and pretended we were Superman.

When we got bored with that, we changed into play clothes and met at the huge tree in Gordon's backyard, which seemed to reach to the heavens. We raced each other up to the tree house his parents had built. We spent hours up there, gazing at the plains all around us while we shared the details of our young lives. In spite of our families' religious differences, my buddy and I had a lot in common. After all, we were both energetic young boys who wanted to make the most of every single day of our lives.

I wished my best friend and I could go to the same school. But as soon as I graduated from kindergarten, Dad enrolled me in Sharona Primary, a private Jewish school. He said he didn't want me to experience the anti-Semitism he'd had to deal with in the public school system. I didn't really understand what he meant—but I guessed that was the point.

A strong gust of wind made the tree house sway. Our eyes widened and we held tight to the furniture, which was nailed to the floor. Though the walls trembled and the floor creaked, we both knew there was no real danger. The trunk was huge and the roots went deep.

On Monday morning, we went our separate ways for the day. As I stood by the living room window, waiting for my carpool ride to school, I considered what words I could use to explain to my classmates how I ended up with only a scrape on my cheek after my dramatic accident, which by now had turned into a big red scab, as I had become known for telling unlikely stories. But this one was true!

I had to tell it really well, especially to convince my friend Lance. That gullible kid believed everything I said. I once found some cool-looking red seeds with a black center, and I told Lance that if he planted one of them and watered it every day, it would grow into a rocket. He believed me and began to diligently water the seed every day! Until his mother noticed him regularly watering something in the yard and asked him what he was doing. When he told her what I'd said, she got mad and called my mom, insisting she make me stop telling her son such yarns.

Of course, I didn't. After all, if Lance was dumb enough to believe that story, I considered it a challenge to see what else I could convince him of.

But Lance wasn't the only kid I enjoyed duping. I had a group of friends who came to our house in Westville to play with me. I told them that if they cut off some of the leafiest boughs of one of our trees, tied them to their arms, stood on the highest chair on our porch, and flapped their arms vigorously, they could fly. I said it with such conviction they believed me. So one by one they climbed onto the chair and flapped their arms and jumped off, only to get bruised and banged up when they hit the ground.

I thought it was hysterical. After all, it wasn't a long fall, and no one got seriously hurt.

"The reason you keep crashing is you aren't flapping hard enough," I told them in my best flight-instructor voice. "Put more effort and energy into it."

After half an hour they got discouraged and we went back to more realistic and less challenging feats, like climbing trees and swimming.

No harm was done, and I'd had a great time. Even at that young age, I was determined that my life would never be boring. Innocent boyish fun added spice to otherwise routine days—for me and for my friends.

THE TALK

After school, I ran home, eager to see Gordon and share with him the story I'd told about the seed growing into a rocket and how that gullible Lance guy had swallowed it hook, line, and sinker.

But before I could get into the house to change into play clothes, my dad stopped me in the backyard. "There's something important we need to discuss," he said in a serious tone.

Great. He'd found out about my fib, and Lance's mother had called again.

Dad took one of the porch chairs and motioned for me to join him. I sat in the adjacent chair, wondering what my punishment would be for my harmless prank.

"Geoff, I know you and Gordon are friends. But the Fletchers are Christians. And sooner or later Christians will always put a knife in your back."

I couldn't imagine my best friend putting a knife in my back, even if my dad did mean it figuratively.

"You remember the Six-Day War, don't you?"

How could I forget the event that rocked my little world just two years ago?

From a very young age, I'd heard horror stories about the Holocaust, when Nazis murdered countless Jews in death camps throughout Europe. Since most Germans claimed to be Catholic or Protestant, we Jews considered Nazis and Christians to be synonymous.

In May of 1948, Holocaust survivors from Europe fought in the War of Independence to get back their ancient homeland. Against impossible odds, they won. After more than two thousand years in exile, the Jews had their freedom and the State of Israel was born.

These stories from history were part of my heritage, something my relatives spoke of often. But generations of persecution became personal in 1967, when I was five years old. For six horrifying days and nights, Muslims in the Arab nations surrounding Israel tried to destroy our homeland.

Though the main conflict took place about five thousand miles away from my home, I was traumatized by the thought even at such a tender young age that if we lost that battle, Jews would not be safe anywhere in the world, including South Africa. Because Israel had become a refuge for persecuted Jews, I felt that the survival of my family, my relatives, and even my own life depended on the Jews winning.

Fortunately, the war lasted only six days. The Jews won a resounding victory with a preemptive strike, annihilating the Egyptian and Arab air force bases. As a result, Jerusalem reverted to Jewish hands for the first time in more than two thousand years.

Even as a seven-year-old, I felt proud to be Jewish, certain that God was with my people. How else could such a tiny nation win so decisively against much larger and better equipped armies? And yet, the cumulative effect of centuries of persecution had left a deep scar on my tender young heart.

"We Jews must stick together," my father said. "This is how we've survived through the centuries."

I wanted to argue in defense of my best friend. Surely Gordon wasn't our enemy. But the look on my father's face and the tone in his voice convinced me not to interrupt.

"When I was a teenager in Johannesburg," he said, "I went camping with a Jewish friend. One night a group of Afrikaans teenagers surrounded our tent. They threw rocks at us and shouted, 'Christ killers!'"

Why in the world would anyone accuse my father of such a thing? Of course we'd heard of the man named Jesus, often called Christ, who'd lived some two thousand years ago. But my dad didn't even know much about the guy. How could anyone accuse him of killing someone who lived in a completely different time and place?

"The world is divided into two groups, Geoff, "us" and "them." You are a Jew, one of God's chosen people." This concept had been ingrained in me from a very young age. I didn't really know what "chosen" meant, but it made me feel special and proud to be Jewish. "Gordon is not one of us. He is one of *them*."

"Are you saying I shouldn't hang around with him anymore?" I asked, my voice shaking. I couldn't imagine not being able to see my best buddy, especially since he lived right next door.

"You can still be friends," Dad said, although I could tell he wasn't comfortable with it. "Just be careful, Son. You can only trust your own people. Remember, it was friendly churchgoers in Europe—much like the Fletchers—who turned in their Jewish neighbors to the Nazis, who then sent them to the Jewish ghettos and even the death camps. We can forgive, but we cannot forget."

I trudged to my room to change clothes. Gordon was waiting for me, and he'd want to know what took me so long to get to the tree house. I couldn't tell him what my father had said. I wasn't sure what I *could* say to him anymore. But after my dad's strong admonition, I knew things would never be quite the same between us.

2

THE MOVE

"I got one!" I squealed as I stood on the deck of my father's company boat, holding on to my fishing pole as tightly as I could. "I bet it's a grunter."

Grunters were delicious. I could practically taste the dish Mom would make when I brought this one home.

With Dad's help, I reeled in my line. But as my big, meaty fish neared the boat, a looming gray shadow appeared. I felt a sharp jerk. The pole nearly flew out of my grip as I pulled in a fish head, its neck in bloody tatters. I dropped my pole and jumped back, sickened by the sight.

This wasn't the first fish head I'd caught. But I never got used to the sight—or to the fear that one day I might fall into those deep waters. The ocean was warm and inviting and great for swimming, surfing, and fishing. But it was also a haven for sharks. As a result of regular attacks, all the major beaches had been skirted with large nets.

In spite of the potential danger and the numerous disappointments, I loved boating on the rough Indian Ocean with my dad and the thrill of the hunt. Even if we didn't catch more than fish heads, it appealed to my sense of adventure.

I'd always admired the Indian fishermen who seemed to have a golden touch when it came to fishing. As I re-baited my hook and put my line back out, I thought about the men who fished at a place called The Bluff, where the Umgeni river met the ocean. It was always murky because of the fresh water entering the sea, and large fish came there to feed—including sharks.

While I watched my line behind the boat, I recalled a time when I was watching an Indian fisherman expertly handle the huge rod he used for deep-sea game fishing. All of a sudden, the pole nearly jerked out of his hands. I heard the screaming of the strong, thick line. Whatever took the bait pulled with such intensity, the fisherman had to release some of the line so he wouldn't be pulled into the ocean.

I wondered if he'd snagged a hammerhead shark or a stingray, both of which were abundant in those waters. I'd heard men talk about five-hour battles to reel in these giants of the ocean.

As this fisherman braced himself for long hours of battle, trying to wear the fish down enough to eventually reel it in, the line snapped as if it were made of cotton. I was disappointed, and certain he was even more so. But not knowing what "monster of the deep" he'd almost caught made the experience all the more intriguing.

I couldn't wait to grow up and become a great fisherman, boater, or surfer myself—maybe even all three!

After Dad brought our boat back to shore, I played at the beach, jumping on the trampoline as high as I could so I could look far out across the ocean at the ships at sea, riding the mighty waves. When I tired of that, I rested on the warm sand, inhaling the smell of coconut suntan oil and listening to the beach vendors shouting, "Ice cream! Lollipops!" in their Indian accent.

I watched the Zulu rickshaw drivers, dressed in animal skins and crowns with huge feathers, taking folks along the coast from one beach to another. They whistled and jumped and ran in bare feet on the hot road, giving the passengers in their two-person carts a thrilling ride.

As always, my attention was diverted by the surfers. I loved watching them ride huge waves as easily as I rode my bike on a winding path. The ocean held a sense of mystique to my boyish imagination. Wondering what mysteries might lurk beneath those waves fascinated me. I dreamed of someday taking up the sport myself.

When the surfers came in for a break between waves, I approached them. "Any chance one of you could teach me how to surf?" I asked, trying to make my high-pitched voice a little deeper so they wouldn't think I was too young.

They talked it over among themselves. Finally one guy asked, "You got a board?"

I dug my toe into the white sand. "No."

He walked up to me and stuck the end of his board into the ground in front of me. "You can learn on mine."

"Really?" My heart raced.

"Sure, why not? Can you be here tomorrow?"

"You bet I can." I stared at the vast ocean. I shuddered when I considered the possibility of being washed out to sea beyond the shark nets. Nevertheless, I was determined to conquer my fears … and the waves.

I raced to my father, eager to tell him the exciting news. But knowing I'd need to convince him to let me do this, I held my tongue as I helped him finish taking care of the boat. All the way home, I rehearsed ways to broach the subject, concerned that the way I presented it would be a huge factor in whether or not he said yes.

SHATTERING NEWS

At dinner that night, I was about to start my well-practiced speech when Dad cleared his throat. "I have an announcement to make." He paused to make sure Barbara and I were paying attention. "I just got a great job offer. I'll be managing a large furniture store in the city. We're relocating to Johannesburg!"

Johannesburg? That concrete jungle six hundred miles from my beautiful ocean, our sunny subtropical paradise, the monkeys—not to mention my friends and my school … and any possibility of learning to surf! Was he kidding?

I wanted to scream. But the eager expression on my dad's face stopped any objections I might have. I knew he had the family's best interests at heart. Johannesburg was the economic capital of the country and he had our long-term future in mind.

This logic did not comfort me at all. I felt nothing but dread and apprehension.

———•———

This wasn't the first time my family had moved.

I was born on February 8, 1962, to Ronald Sydney Cohen and Zena Cohen in a small town called Vryheid, in what is now Kwazulu, Natal. Barely enough Jewish families lived there to hold a *minyan*, which according to the Jewish faith is the minimum of ten people required for a synagogue service. Back then Vryheid was a coal-mining town of about five thousand people. My grandfather owned a furniture store, which my dad had taken over.

Shortly after I was born, in keeping with generations of Jewish tradition, my parents consulted with my grandparents to find me a Jewish name. They chose Yankel Lazer Cohen. Yankel is the Yiddish version of Jacob, which means "to grab by the heel." Lazer, from the Hebrew Eleazer, means "God is my help." Both of these names turned out to be prophetic in describing my life's journey.

After giving me my original Jewish name, my parents had to find a modern English equivalent since we were no longer in a Jewish shtetl in Eastern Europe. They came up with the name I am known by today, Geoffrey Lance Cohen.

When I was fifteen months old, my father was transferred to Durban to run a furniture store for a much larger company. Durban was a beautiful subtropical port city on the warm Indian Ocean, with gorgeous beaches and great surf.

We lived in an apartment at first. I hated it. According to my mother, I sat at the door every morning, screaming to go outside. As soon as she opened the door, I stopped crying and flew outdoors to play. I spent so much time outside, my skin became brown as a berry and the soles of my feet got rough and calloused from running around barefoot all the time.

Mom says I've always hated being in confined spaces, even before I was born. She got pregnant with me when Barbie was two, much sooner than she and Dad had planned. Her labor with me lasted less than an hour. She said it seemed like I couldn't wait to escape from the darkness I'd been swirling around in for nine months and get into the real world where I could enjoy the adventures of life.

After a year in that apartment, my parents bought an acre of land with huge trees in the yard, several of which were great for climbing and building tree houses. My dad built a huge pool, which provided hours of fun for me. I learned to swim at a very early age, and I spent hours diving, splashing, swimming laps, and playing Marco Polo with my sisters and my friends.

Durban was a kid's paradise, with boundless opportunities for an adventurous young boy like me. Johannesburg represented the loss of that paradise and the death of my happy childhood.

PATCH

A few days before we were scheduled to leave Durban, my parents bought me a dog. "She's a cross between a British corgi and a bull terrier," Dad said.

She was built like a bull terrier: short, stocky, and muscular. She was totally white except for a brown patch of fur around her right eye—the only giveaway that she was not a thoroughbred. So I named her Patch.

Most families in our neighborhood had at least two dogs, usually big, strong ones for security reasons. We'd had our share as well. Patch was pretty little in comparison. But a smaller dog would probably be better for city living.

"Bull terriers are one-owner pets," Mom told me. "They are very loyal and extremely protective of their masters." She knelt down beside me as I stroked the animal's back, her tail wagging a mile a minute. "I'd say Patch has chosen you to be her master."

I took the squirmy ball of fur into my arms. This new friend was exactly what I needed in my transition to a new environment, which I perceived would be harsh and unfriendly.

"Can she sleep on my bed?" I asked.

My parents hesitated, but talked it over and finally agreed. When I crawled under my thick, heavy comforter, Patch jumped onto my bed, licked my face, and curled up at my feet. From that point on, my bed was hers. And the two of us were inseparable.

PARADISE LOST

My heart broke every time I said good-bye to one of my friends, the Zulus I loved, the Indian fishermen I enjoyed hanging out with, Rosie, even my teachers. The day before we left Durban, I rode my bike to my favorite places, knowing I would probably never see them again. I went to the ocean and watched the surfers from a distance, wondering what they thought about the little boy who begged for lessons and then never showed up to take them.

Our first home in Johannesburg was a townhouse. Although Dad promised it was temporary, I hated it. I missed our huge backyard and pool. I missed the almost constant sunshine of Durban. And I detested having to wear shoes.

Back home, I'd run around barefoot a lot, so my feet had become calloused and tough. But Johannesburg winters were too cold to go without shoes. Plus I knew the city kids would think I was weird if they saw me outdoors barefoot. Still, I despised the idea that my soles would become soft if I wore shoes all the time. And "soft feet" represented the loss of the rugged existence I'd left behind. I didn't want to become a big-city kid.

Patch didn't like the townhouse any better than I did. She spent most of her time with her paws on the windowsill in the living room, whining. Since I was afraid she might get lost, she could only go outside on a leash, which she wasn't used to at all.

There was no going back, so we both had to make the best of it. I begrudgingly determined to adapt to my new environment, no matter how much of an uphill battle it turned out to be.

After a short time in the townhouse, we moved to a nice suburb called Bramley North. It was a predominantly middle- to upper-middle-class Jewish neighborhood. We had a large plot of land with a decent-sized house. The backyard had a sauna and a pool, which was barely long enough to swim laps in. At the bottom of our yard, stone steps on a steep hill led to a garden with a huge mulberry tree, a fig tree, a plum tree, and lots of other fruit trees.

Though this place paled in comparison to our home in Durban, at least it had a fenced-in yard with enough room for Patch to run around.

Directly behind our backyard, below the fruit trees, was an Anglican church. The huge neon cross on top of its steeple glowed in the dark and could be seen from quite far away. It reminded me of the nightmarish pogroms my grandfather told me about. Those stories, seared in my young mind, made me hate that cross. To me it represented death, hatred of Jews, and persecution. I was convinced that every Sunday Christians listened to a priest rant on about how evil the Jews were.

Their book, the New Testament—which Jews were forbidden to read—apparently claimed that Jesus was the Son of God and that Jews had done horrible things, including killing their Savior. Of course, we didn't believe that. But I guessed that was why they hated us so much.

In spite of how Christians had treated Jews over the centuries, we never returned evil for evil. We just wanted to live at peace with them. But clearly the feeling was not always mutual.

Most of the kids on our street went to the same private Jewish school: King David, in Linksfield.

There were two non-Jewish families on our street. We didn't interact with them much. One of the families had a son a few years older than me, and a daughter about Barbie's age. One day, I was riding my bike down the sidewalk and the daughter shoved a large branch between the spokes of my front wheel, then ran off. Fortunately, I managed to scramble onto my feet as the bike tipped; otherwise, I could have been badly hurt.

I wondered why anyone would do such a thing.

It reminded me of the day I came home from school in Durban and saw a group of kids I didn't know gathered around a tree. As I got closer, I saw that they were throwing stones at a cute little vervet monkey. I was furious and very upset, but too young to do anything about it. I ran home and told my father what I'd seen. "Bullies are usually cowards," he said. I vowed to protect the innocent and the helpless from bullies whenever I could.

Maybe my dad was right. Jews really did need to stick together because Christians couldn't be trusted.

———•———

Back in Durban, the moms had taken turns driving all the kids in the neighborhood to school and back. Here I'd have to ride to school in a big bus with back-to-back benches and poles for students who couldn't get seats to hold on to. The nearest bus stop was a mile-long walk away.

My first day on the bus, I was nervous about being the new kid. As I boarded, one of the older students asked me where I came from.

"I'm from Durban."

"Oh, so you're a banana boy!" he said in a mocking, derogatory tone.

The reminder of my hometown, where banana trees grew wild and monkeys scampered in the trees, made me want to cry. I also got the message loud and clear. Because I was not a big-city kid, I didn't fit in here.

From that point on, the kids on the bus bullied me every day. I didn't know how to deal with that. So home became my refuge, my sanctuary.

And Patch became my hero. I was the new kid on the block, being bullied on the bus by kids bigger than me. Patch was shorter than most dogs in the neighborhood, but no one could mess with her. Those who tried ended up regretting it. Patch was like the Mike Tyson of dogs, and I wanted to be the Mike Tyson of my world too.

Patch had incredible hunting instincts. One day, when I came home from school, I saw six dead sparrows scattered over our yard. I couldn't imagine how they could have died. There were no bullet holes in their bodies, and they were so small and fast it was almost impossible to shoot one with a pellet gun.

I went into the house, and when I looked out the window to the side yard, I saw Patch standing as still as a statue, not twitching a muscle. A sparrow was right in front of her on the grass, innocently looking for bugs, unaware that a bull terrier stood less than a foot away. Suddenly, as fast as lightning, Patch grabbed the bird in her mouth, crushed the life out of it, held it a bit longer to make sure it was dead, then dropped it and waited for the next unsuspecting bird victim. That explained all the dead birds in our yard!

Birds weren't Patch's only prey. At one point we had a problem with rats in our yard. The wooden shed where we kept our lawn mower, fertilizer, and garden equipment was a rat's paradise. They also loved to hang out in the eight-foot-by-four-foot brick shed near the back of the house, where we stored coal for the winter fireplace and for barbeques. It had a heavy metal top, and there was a small opening on the ground level of the rectangular brick structure, just big enough for a spade to fit in so the coal could be shoveled into a wheelbarrow.

I had a distinct whistle that Patch recognized. No matter how far away she was, when I whistled, she came running to wherever I was. One day after school, I whistled and whistled, but Patch didn't show up. I looked everywhere I could think of. I even had neighbors join in the search. Finally, I went to the coal shed, lifted the heavy metal cover, and there she was, my snow-white dog, as black as the ace of spades, standing in that same motionless posture I'd seen when she was hunting for sparrows. In front of her was a high, neatly stacked pyramid of dead rats.

The minute a little rat's head poked out from the coal pile to see if the coast was clear, Patch snatched the unsuspecting rodent by the head, pulled it out, broke its neck, and added it to the mountain of carcasses. Patch looked out for us in every way.

One day, just for fun, I bought some stink bombs from a toy store.

The label on the sealed vial promised that when the glass shattered, the contents would give off a putrid, sulfur-like smell. I could hardly wait to use it.

I walked nonchalantly to the home of our neighbor two doors down. I looked around to make sure the coast was clear. From the driveway, I looked up at the window of the bathroom. It was open and I saw some movement inside. I crept up to the window, threw the vial in, and heard it shatter. Bull's-eye!

Without waiting for a response, I ran back up their driveway. Just before I got to the top, an adult jumped out from behind the bushes and grabbed my arm.

He must have been watching me, just waiting to catch me in the act.

I tried to pull away from his grip on my arm, but he was too strong. As he yanked me toward the house, I knew I was in for a beating.

At that moment Patch appeared at the top of our driveway. Perfect timing.

"Let me go," I shouted, loud enough for Patch to hear, and struggled like the guy was about to murder me.

Patch ran at him, ears back, as silent and deadly as a torpedo racing toward a ship. I could tell she wanted to rip this guy to pieces for daring to touch her "sweet, innocent" master.

The neighbor quickly let go of my arm, ran into the house, and slammed the front door behind him just in time.

I went home, profusely thanking my dog for coming to my rescue, but nervous as to what would happen the next time this man saw me, especially if I was alone.

A few days later, he saw me while I was playing in our front yard. Looking around nervously, he asked, "How's your dog doing?"

"She's very well. Thanks for asking."

Confident that he was not going to get me in trouble, I decided never to throw another stink bomb at his home.

ROBSON

Shortly after our move to Bramley North, my parents hired a domestic worker named Robson. Most middle- to upper-middle-class families employed two domestic workers: a male for the gardening and property maintenance, and a female for the kitchen work, housework, and cooking. We always treated our servants like part of the family, and Robson was no exception.

Robson was from the Matabele tribe, which traced their ancestry to the cream of the Zulu warriors, who carried an air of immortality about them. Robson personified the values and principles of a Zulu warrior. He was a regal and imposing figure, built like a prizefighter. But he was soft spoken and dignified, and he soon became my new best friend.

I spent more time in the servants' quarters part of the house with him than I did in the main house with my mom and dad. My parents were good people and great providers, but they let us kids fend for ourselves and find our own paths in life. Dad traveled a lot on business trips and was highly work oriented, and Mom was very active socially. I gleaned a lot from my parents, who had many wonderful qualities. But just as I had felt nurtured by Rosie, our Zulu servant in Durban, I learned many of my values and life principles from Robson.

———•———

For my tenth birthday, my father bought me a pellet gun. I used the single-shot air rifle to shoot at tin cans and other targets. I loved the *ting* sound the soda cans made as I hit them, just before they were knocked over. I engaged in a few shooting competitions with other kids in the neighborhood and usually won.

One of my favorite evening pastimes was shooting at the cross atop the church steeple behind our backyard. It was always illuminated at night and could be seen from miles away. I considered it a real eyesore, especially being in such a predominantly Jewish neighborhood as ours. Of course, the range of my pellet gun was nowhere near sufficient, so I never achieved my goal of seeing the light of the cross extinguished.

One of my neighborhood Jewish friends, Gary, also had a pellet gun, so we sometimes went shooting together in my backyard. One day we got bored of shooting cans and cereal boxes and decided to go to the Jukskei River to look for frogs or birds to shoot. Strolling along the bank of the stream, we felt like real hunters. We never actually killed any birds, because the crack of the bullets scared them off. But we had fun anyway.

On our way back home, we took a shortcut by climbing under a big hole in the fence around the church property. Just before we got to the fence behind my house, we bumped into the priest. "What have you boys been doing with those guns?" he demanded.

I stared at his red face over his black robe and white collar, unable to speak. He looked just like I envisioned the Orthodox priest in my grandfather's pogrom stories.

"You've been shooting birds, haven't you?" His bushy eyebrows scrunched together.

"No, sir," Gary said. "They were too far away and too fast for our guns to hit." He grinned. "We did kill some large frogs, though." His chest puffed up with pride over our accomplishment.

The priest scolded us, loudly, for several minutes.

I was too frightened to really hear his words, but the impression I got was that this angry, self-righteous, holier-than-thou man had the opportunity to give my friend and me a positive impression of how Christians saw Jews, and even to share words of eternal life with us, but instead he chose to chastise us for shooting animals. Weren't two young Jewish boys more important to his God than frogs and birds? Apparently not. I vowed never to grace the doors of a Christian church as long as I lived.

3

HEARTBREAK

When I was twelve years old, I came home from school one day, tossed my book satchel into my room, and went outside to call for Patch. She did not come to greet me. I figured she must be catching rats, hunting birds, or rummaging through a neighbor's trash cans.

None of our Jewish neighbors minded Patch getting into their garbage. We all knew each other and accepted that was how dogs were. And Patch was never aggressive unless she was provoked or protecting the family.

The Sands, however—the only Christians in the neighborhood besides the family with the daughter who shoved a branch between the spokes of my front bike wheel—did complain. They never communicated with my parents directly, but Robson told us several times that the Sands' domestic gardener had come to him, insisting he stop Patch from rummaging through their trash. I heard through the grapevine that they'd even made vague threats against our family if we didn't comply.

My parents ignored the third-party warnings. After all, we couldn't stop our dog from going to their house. She loved her freedom, and she would never hurt or attack anyone or anything, except in self-defense or to protect me, her master.

I whistled the special code that only Patch and I understood. Still no response. I looked everywhere for her, including the shed where she hunted rats and the coal storage area where she liked to play, but found no sign of her.

Getting a really bad feeling, I began looking under bushes. When I checked a bush near our garage, I saw Patch lying there. "Hey, girl," I called, excited to have found her. But she didn't move. My dog was dead!

I sank to my knees and wailed. Robson came running. When he saw Patch, he picked her up gently. "We can take her to the vet," he said in his thick accent and gravelly voice. "She might still be alive."

But I knew better. Rigor mortis had set in, and her body was already stiff.

"I hate Johannesburg," I screamed, then stumbled to my room and flopped onto the bed. I wept so hard I could barely breathe. I'd left all my friends and everything familiar to come to this horrible place. Patch had been one of the only redemptive elements that made this move bearable, and now she was gone too.

My family had always had dogs. But Patch was "mine." She was irreplaceable. No other pet would ever be able to fill this hole in my heart.

When I ran out of tears to shed, I blew my nose and sat up in bed, wondering how this tragedy could have happened.

Then it hit me. The Sands must have poisoned her!

Rage filled my heart. Was that all Christians knew how to do, just kill and destroy things? Our Jewish neighbors would never dream of poisoning a dog.

But how to prove it? A vet could do an autopsy. But I couldn't bear the thought of Patch getting cut open and going through tests. Better to let her rest in peace. Besides, even if I could prove foul play, what was the point? My closest companion was gone forever, and nothing was going to change that. I decided not to stoop to their level and let hatred poison my soul.

All I could do was hope there was a dog heaven, where Patch and I could someday be reunited.

For weeks after her death, my life was a blur. I went through the motions of waking up, eating breakfast, putting on my school uniform, catching the bus to school. I endured the teasing and bullying without response, attended classes without listening to the instructor, ate sandwiches on my own during lunch, sat alone on the grass at recess, caught the bus back, walked to my house, did my homework, had dinner, then went to bed early, repeating the same routine day after day.

Every reminder of Patch caused such deep pain, I got rid of all the photos I had of her.

After a few months of this morose behavior, my dad took me to a man who bred prize-winning Labrador retrievers. "These pups are of top British stock," he told us. "Their grandfather won many awards for being such a perfect thoroughbred."

Dad told me to pick the one I liked best. "But get a male this time."

I was drawn to a cute little black male who had an even cuter golden sister. They seemed inseparable, rolling, frolicking, and playing with each other.

I gazed up at my father with pleading eyes. "Can we get them both?" I begged. "Please?"

My tenderhearted, generous father relented and bought them both. I called the black dog Merlin and the golden dog Vicky.

Raising two young puppies kept me very busy over the next several months. And having something to pour my affections into made the loss of Patch a bit more bearable.

When Merlin grew bigger, he went hunting and swimming with

me. We chased ducks on the lake for hours and went on long walks in the bush together. Though he could never replace Patch, he was a great companion.

ROBSON, MY BEST FRIEND

Robson, however, remained my closest friend. After school and on weekends, we sat in the servants' quarters and talked for hours. Though he was not formally educated, he was one of the best communicators I have ever known. His stories about the war in Zimbabwe (which was Rhodesia at that time, and under British colonial rule), tribal culture, and African life in general held me spellbound. He spoke slowly, deliberately, with long pauses for effect, and I hung on his every word. The mental images he painted transported me to the times and places he talked about, and I eagerly took in the sights, smells, sounds, tastes, and colors.

Due to apartheid, Robson and his wife, Phyllis, had to live in separate houses. She worked as a domestic servant for a family who lived about a mile away from us. They both had to have a "pass," like a visa, to work in a white area, and if they didn't keep it updated with the police, they could be imprisoned. They couldn't go to "white" beaches or movie houses, or use public transportation. Even public restrooms were divided: one for blacks and one for whites.

The vast majority of the Jewish community supported the abolition of the apartheid system and many actively campaigned against it, sometimes at the risk of their physical safety and even their lives.

My father used his position as a successful and influential business leader to help bring about change. He employed store managers of many races in his company. He promoted people based on their skills, regardless of their color. Some pro-apartheid Afrikaans conservatives threatened his life for his stand against apartheid, but he held his ground. I was proud of my dad's accomplishments and his fight for equal rights for all.

Though Robson and his wife saw each other regularly, he was quite a womanizer. Once, he confided in me that he had six children from different girlfriends in various townships. They were all boys, and he had named every one of them Geoffrey, after me. In spite of my disagreement with his moral choices, that made me feel special.

Since I had few friends at school, the fact that Robson always had time for me helped to build in me a tremendous sense of self-worth. He made me feel that I was worth investing time in. When we were together, nothing seemed more important to him than I was.

One evening, as Robson and I sat in his room, talking, I pointed at his bed, which sat on four tall metal legs resting on clay bricks. All of my black African friends had beds like that, but Robson's was so high off the ground, only a very tall person could get into it without standing on a chair. I thought it quite inconvenient, especially if he had to go to the restroom in the middle of the night. "Why is your bed so high?" I asked.

"That is to keep the Tokolosh from getting onto my bed," he said as if it were an obvious fact of life.

"What's a Tokolosh?"

"It is a vicious little monkey-like creature with very sharp teeth. It is quite short, so it cannot climb up the bricks under my bed and bite me while I am sleeping."

The vervet monkeys in Durban were short and had sharp teeth, but I'd never heard of one getting into people's beds and biting them. And I'd never seen any monkeys in Johannesburg. I concluded that this creature must be fictitious.

To the indigenous blacks in South Africa, the spiritual world seemed more real than the visible world. Many of these people practiced ancestor worship and witchcraft, resulting in a great deal of fear and superstition.

"How come I've never seen one of these creatures?" I asked.

"That is because you are white," he answered matter-of-factly. "They are afraid of white people, so they only attack black people."

"Do you know anyone who has actually been bitten by a Tokolosh?"

"Absolutely," he replied in a serious tone. "A friend of mine, whose bed was not high enough, got bite marks all over his neck. He could have died. But he went to a witch doctor and spent all he had on a spell and a potion to keep the Tokolosh away. And they never bothered him again."

Okay, this was getting creepy. And boy, was I glad to be white, which apparently kept the Tokolosh away from me!

While I didn't understand how a person could be scared of something he'd never seen, I realized this was a very real part of Robson's daily life, and I didn't want to trivialize it. If I came across as patronizing, it could affect our valuable friendship. So I accepted his explanation.

Robson was a friendly, fun-loving guy, but he was also an incredible fighter, and he was afraid of no one. He lived by the principle that if you called someone your friend, you would be loyal to him unto death. If you weren't willing to die for the person you called your friend, you had no right to call him friend.

This was a value system handed down to him from generations of mighty Zulu warriors and I cherished it. The concept of loyalty, even unto death, seemed unique in the midst of a rather shallow Western culture where most people were mainly concerned about what others could do for them.

Once, when Robson and I were sitting in his room talking, he stopped in midsentence and looked me in the eye as if he were about to say something very important. Then, in his thick Matabele accent, he said, "Geoff, you and me, we live together as brothers and we will die for each other if need be." That was his way of making a covenant with me, promising that he would be my friend forever.

In the Zulu and Matabele culture, making a covenant with someone was the highest act of loyalty and devotion. Robson had obviously thought this through.

For a white kid and a black man to be best friends represented a great risk for us both. I felt honored that he would make this covenant with me, knowing it could cost him his life.

Once, it almost did.

One evening, the two of us walked to the shops together. By the time we started for home, it was after nine p.m. Two policemen stopped us and asked him for his passbook to prove he was allowed to be in a "white" area. He showed it to them and they saw it was in order.

The taller one peered at me. "Does your father know you're hanging out with a black man alone late at night in the streets?"

"Not only does he know, he fully encourages our friendship."

"Oh, really? Well, then, you must be a communist."

Robson's huge, calloused hands balled into fists. "Geoffrey," he seethed, "please let me beat them up!"

I grabbed his sleeve. "Stay calm," I whispered back. "They're just trying to provoke you into a fight so they'll have an excuse to shoot you."

Robson stood still, though he did not release his fists. I breathed a sigh of relief, knowing that if my friend so much as took a step toward the officers, they would feel justified in attacking him, possibly even killing him.

Since the police had no legal charge to hold us for, they had to let us go our way. I thanked God for protecting my best friend's life.

A few weeks later, Robson came home covered in blood. I asked what happened, and he said he'd been drinking in an illegal African bar called a shebeen that served a version of moonshine. While he was there he had a run in with some guys who didn't know his reputation and were dumb enough to pick a fight with him.

"You should go to the hospital immediately."

"No," he answered in his deep, gravelly voice. "I was not hurt." He pointed at his clothes. "This is the blood of the other men!" He took off his shirt. After he'd washed his body, I saw that he didn't have a scratch on him.

Another time, Robson went to a convenience store in town, and when he came out, six guys with huge cowboy knives tried to mug him. He fought back in self-defense. For a good twenty minutes, Robson fought for his life, skillfully avoiding the long blades and punching his adversaries whenever he saw an opening.

When the store owner saw the battle, he called the police. They broke up the fight. The other guys, who were bruised and bleeding, claimed that Robson had attacked them. Of course their accusation didn't stick. No one would be crazy enough to believe that one unarmed guy had attacked six men with huge knives.

During the apartheid days, only whites were allowed to get a license to carry a firearm. One of the few exceptions was for black police officers who had proven their loyalty to the Afrikaans-dominated regime. These ruthless oppressors treated their own people even harsher than the white-Afrikaans police officers. They couldn't even live among their own people because they were considered traitors.

One day, my father got a phone call from the police, saying that Robson had been in a fight and had been arrested. I asked Dad to let me go see him. When I visited my friend in jail, he told me what happened.

The previous evening, Robson was walking on the sidewalk beside a main road and came upon two black policemen, talking. Instead of going around them, which would mean stepping into traffic on the busy street, Robson politely asked the officers if they would please move out of the way so he could pass by.

The officers glared at him. "So, you're cheeky, huh?" one asked, basically saying, *How dare you question my authority?*

"Not at all," Robson replied calmly. "I just want to get past you."

Without warning, the officer struck him on the forehead with his thick wooden baton, opening a gash in his head. When he tried to strike again, Robson raised his arm to protect himself, and the baton slashed his elbow. As he bled profusely from his head and his elbow, the other officer joined in the attack.

Robson struck back in a furious rage. Though he could only see the police officers through his own blood, he beat them both up in a short span of time, then stood back to catch his breath.

During the struggle, one officer's handgun had fallen out of its holster and landed in the grass. Even though Robson had stopped fighting, the officer picked up his weapon, took six steps back, and shot at him three times.

One bullet went into his left thigh and lodged in his buttock; another entered his waist just below his rib cage and went out the other side. A third bullet hit an innocent bystander who, I heard later, was crippled for the rest of his life because he just happened to be in the wrong place at the wrong time.

Robson was taken to a hospital, where he had to stand in line, under police supervision, all the while losing blood. When he finally got to the front of the line, a doctor removed the bullet without using any anesthetic. After the other wounds were cleaned, Robson was thrown into jail to recover from his injuries while he awaited trial on the charge of assaulting police officers with intent to do grievous bodily harm.

I was devastated at the thought of possibly losing my best friend. But I was even more concerned for him.

Robson was so enraged by the idea of black policemen betraying their own people, he wanted to beat up every officer he saw. Whenever one of the guards passed his cell, he screamed, "You black dogs and you white dogs are all the same!" When a guard gave him food, he reached through the bars and tried to grab him so he could strangle him.

As a result of his violent attitude and behavior, Robson was transferred to a private cell reserved for the most dangerous of prisoners, with guards pushing his food through a metal plate under the door.

Eventually he calmed down and was put back into the main jail with the rest of the inmates.

Because of his reputation as a fighter, the judge deemed Robson a danger to society and determined that his fists were lethal weapons. For the safety of everyone, he decided to "limit" Robson's hands. That meant my friend would have to undergo an operation in which the tendons of both of his hands would be surgically damaged so he could not make a fist.

I knew if that happened, Robson would not want to live. He took tremendous pride in his strength and fighting ability. After all, was that not the reason he was still alive?

I told my father everything Robson shared with me. I begged him to find a lawyer to represent our servant so he would not be sentenced to prison or have the tendons in his hands surgically damaged.

My dad hired the best lawyer money could buy. At the trial Robson was vindicated and his hands were not "limited," thank God. The police officers who assaulted him were transferred to another station, not as punishment but out of their concern for their safety.

This experience changed Robson, though the differences were not obvious to those who didn't know him as well as I did. He was more withdrawn and not as happy-go-lucky as he used to be. He drank more and bordered on becoming an alcoholic.

On one occasion, after he'd had a few too many beers as we were drinking together, he looked at the floor and muttered, "I am just a *kaffir*." This was the worst racial slur used in South Africa in those days, similar to "the n word" in the US. Racists used it in everyday conversation with one another, but only spoke it directly to a black man if they wanted to provoke him.

I was horrified that my best friend would say such a thing about himself, much less feel that way. "That is the most horrible lie you could ever believe. You are the most incredible person I know." My eyes pooled with tears. Before me sat a broken man, stripped of his dignity and pride, believing that he was not equal to me just because he wasn't white. At that moment I hated the Afrikaaners and their apartheid system for doing such a horrible thing to this wonderful man and thousands of others who had been dehumanized by the apartheid system.

I realized Robson was not perfect. But he had given me valuable friendship and unwavering loyalty. He was willing to die for me, a young Jewish white kid, simply because I was his friend. I knew other people who didn't have affairs, drink, or fight, but most of them were self-righteous, prejudiced, judgmental, and far too busy to spend time with a kid like me. This one-of-a-kind man was irreplaceable. Surely he was a gift from God to me during some of the hardest days of my life.

4

MY FAITH

From a very young age, I always had a strong faith in the God of Israel. My last name, Cohen, which is the Hebrew word for "priest," descends from the original priestly tribe of Levi. As Cohanim men, my father and I were highly honored in the community, and especially in the synagogue.

Because of our priestly ancestry, my dad and I were not allowed be defiled by coming close to a dead body. We had to stand within fifty feet of the grave at any funeral in a Jewish cemetery. I considered that a benefit, because I hated going to Jewish funerals. I found them depressing because there was such finality to them.

As I stood with my father fifty feet away at my uncle's funeral, I wondered where he was now. Did his life simply end after death, or did he go somewhere else? Judaism did not seem to give a clear and definitive answer to this deeply personal and important question. I was relieved to watch from a distance as everyone cried and mourned while the coffin was lowered into the grave.

My family attended a traditional, orthodox synagogue, where the entire service was in Hebrew with the exception of the sermon. We followed along in our Siddur, which is our Hebrew prayer book with prayers and order of service. Some of the prayers are thousands of years old.

The women sat upstairs; the men sat downstairs, close to the huge, beautiful bimah (the raised platform from which the Torah was read) and near the ark that contained the Holy Scriptures.

Once everyone was seated, our chazzan ascended the stairs to the platform to recite a portion of the Torah. He was a huge man who looked even bigger with his large prayer shawl wrapped around him.

The chazzan chanted from the Torah, and he had an incredible baritone singing voice. A choir responded in Hebrew from a room behind the veil, high above the bimah. Since they couldn't be seen, it seemed as if their voices came straight from heaven.

After the reading of the Torah, our rabbi took the chazzan's place to preach the message.

All the formal traditions practiced in my synagogue created a sense of awe and grandeur to me as a preadolescent.

After I turned thirteen and had my bar mitzvah, I would occasionally be asked to make *aliyah*, a Hebrew word that literally means "to go up" or "to ascend." This great honor was equivalent to "ascending" spiritually to the Word of God. That meant I could read from the Torah in the synagogue with the other men and even, on special occasions, carry it. Because I was a direct descendent of Aaron, like my father, I would have this great honor more often than most. I looked forward to the day when I would be officially considered a man.

When the rabbi raised his hands, everyone stood simultaneously and chanted the Shema together, slowly and deliberately, a cappella: *Shema Yisrael, Adonai Ehloheinu, Adonai Echad.* "Hear, O Israel, the Lord our God, the Lord is one." This is a declaration of the Jewish faith in the one true God: the God of Abraham, Isaac, and Jacob—the Creator of the universe.

The Shema resounded strongly with me. If there was one statement of faith I knew and believed in, it was that. It made perfect sense to me and I never questioned it.

Though I had never been in a Christian church, and was too scared to even enter one, I had heard that Christians bowed down and prayed to statues of Mary and various saints. The thought horrified me. This practice seemed so idolatrous, it made me even more determined never to worship any god but the one true God of Israel.

During the synagogue services, I could feel God's holiness, much as I did on Friday nights when we had the Shabbat meal at home and my mother lit the Sabbath candles and my father said the blessing over the wine and bread.

To me, God seemed unreachable and rather impersonal. I saw his hand in the big picture, preserving the Jewish people and looking out for us. But I figured he was too busy with the really important stuff to be involved in the details of anyone's personal life. My knowledge of Jewish history had taught me that God got angry when people didn't follow all of his rules. Considering how many times my ancestors had been persecuted and killed over the centuries, he was obviously mad at us a lot.

I hoped he wasn't angry with me personally. But since he was omniscient, he knew about all the stunts I'd pulled in my life. Like telling Lance those mysterious-looking seeds would become a rocket if he planted them and watered them regularly. Or convincing those kids that they could fly if they strapped big leaves to their backs and flapped really hard.

I was guilty of other pranks as well. Like putting itching powder down people's backs and then roaring with laughter while they went berserk trying to scratch. Or throwing a stink bomb into the open bathroom window of our neighbor's house. Or making random phone calls to numbers I found in the phone book and telling whoever answered that I'd lost my mommy, begging them to help me find her. I even recorded those prank calls and played them back to my friends and had a big laugh at those people's expense. To me this was all innocent, boyish fun that added some spice to otherwise routine school days. However, as I sat in synagogue, I couldn't help but wonder whether holy and almighty God saw my schemes more seriously and had plans to punish me for them someday.

Though we celebrated the Sabbath every Friday night as a family at home, we didn't attend synagogue every week. But we were always there for the High Holy Days—Rosh Hashanah (the Feast of Trumpets) and Yom Kippur (the Day of Atonement)—as well as most of the other festivals, including Shavuot (commemorating the day God gave the Torah to the nation of Israel at Mount Sinai) and Sukkoth (the Feast of Tabernacles). Many of the major annual festivals were also celebrated at my Jewish school.

One of my favorite holidays was Purim, which celebrates the Jewish victory when Haman declared a day on which all the Jews should be killed, but the Jewish Queen Esther interceded with the king, and the Jews were saved and Haman was hanged on the gallows that were prepared for her uncle Mordecai. On that holiday all the students dressed up as the various players in the drama. The teacher read the book of Esther, and every time the name Haman was mentioned we all hissed and shook the rattlers we were given to block out his name. To commemorate our victory and his defeat, we ate hamantaschen, a delicious triangular pastry with a sweet filling made of poppy seeds or cream cheese. *Hamantaschen* means "Haman's ears" in Yiddish, the language spoken by all Jews in Europe before Israel became a nation again. So we were symbolically eating the ears of our defeated enemy. I thought this was cool, especially since those ears tasted mighty good!

I also loved Chanukah, which celebrates the Jewish victory over the Syro-Phoenicians under Antiochus Epiphanies after they desecrated the temple in Jerusalem and forced the Jews to worship a statue of the Greek god Zeus. Judah Maccabee and his Jewish warriors defeated the mightiest empire on earth over a period of a few years, then cleansed and rededicated the temple to God. I admired the Maccabees for their courage to stand up for God and Israel. I aspired to do something heroic like that myself one day.

My favorite service of the year was Simchat Torah, which means the "rejoicing of the law." This is an annual celebration of the completion of the reading of the Torah for that year. At this most joyful of all the Jewish holidays, rabbis carry on their shoulders the Torah and dance around the bimah.

I loved watching grown men rejoicing in the synagogue. This was the only time of the year they actually seemed happy and joyful during the service.

When I grew older I would be allowed to participate in the celebration. Every week I could touch the Torah with my Siddur and kiss it, symbolizing my reverence for God's Word. But on Simchat Torah I could carry the huge, heavy Torah on my shoulders. Having direct contact with it would make me feel big and strong, like a real man. I hoped it would also bring me a bit closer to God.

To end the Simchat Torah celebration, the rabbis threw chocolate candy at all us kids. I gathered up as many pieces as I could. I loved chocolate—even the kosher kind. And I loved this holiday because it gave me hope that maybe God wasn't always angry. Perhaps, on these special occasions when he saw us rejoicing in his Word, he might actually be pleased.

My least favorite holiday was Yom Kippur, the Day of Atonement. Between Rosh Hashanah (the Jewish New Year according to the Hebrew calendar) and Yom Kippur were the Days of Awe, a ten-day period of introspection and prayer when everyone was supposed to go to the synagogue regularly to seek God and reevaluate our lives. According to Jewish tradition, it is during this time when God decides whether or not your name will be in the Book of Life for the coming year. This decision is based on whether your good deeds outweighed your bad deeds, how repentant you were over your bad deeds, how often you prayed, and how often you performed mitzvoth, the Hebrew term for charitable deeds. Basically, the degree to which you kept God's commandments determined whether you were a good person and a good Jew in God's sight.

Personally, I found the whole process depressing and even a little scary. Since I had no clue how to determine whether or not I made the grade, how could I have any assurance either way? I felt like I was a pretty good boy, to the best of my knowledge, but I wasn't sure if God felt the same way about me.

At the end of this ten-day period, on the Day of Atonement, we fasted from all food for twenty-four hours. I hated this time of year because I loved food. All day long I would dream about what I was going to eat when we broke our fast and had a great feast.

My parents didn't talk about God much, but they followed the traditions Jews have held to for thousands of years. I have no doubt they did it all with the utmost sincerity and with a desire to please God.

KING DAVID SCHOOL

My instruction about God and his ways came mostly from my private Jewish school. Every Friday morning all the students and teachers assembled on a large tarmac in the back of the school, facing two flags: the Israeli flag and the South African flag. We stood in neat formation in our uniforms and sang the South African national anthem in Afrikaans while the first flag was raised. The translation of this patriotic song includes these lyrics: "We will answer your call, we will offer whatever you ask of us, we will live, we will starve for you, South Africa." While the second flag was raised, we sang the Israeli national anthem, "Hatikvah" (which means "The Hope"), in Hebrew.

Singing these two anthems every week from age ten to twelve created a serious dilemma in my young mind as I pondered my identity as a South African Jew. Was my first loyalty to Israel or to South Africa?

After three years at King David primary school in Johannesburg, I entered junior high at the age of twelve. The assemblies continued, as did the teasing and bullying on the bus trips.

But my art teacher, Mrs. Schlapobersky, believed in me. I enjoyed painting and sketching, and I got high grades for my artwork.

One day after school, I used charcoal to sketch my golden Labrador, Vicky, sitting on my bed. I carefully copied her features, bit by bit, until I had her whole form on the sketchpad. When it was completed, it actually looked like my dog. I was amazed and excited at the same time.

A few months later, Mrs. Schlapobersky was replaced with another teacher, who said I couldn't draw or paint at all and that I had no potential as an artist. I was crushed. I lost all confidence in my artistic ability, and I never drew again.

Recess was lonely for me. Since I had no friends, I ate my packed lunch on my own. I couldn't wait for the day to be over so I could go back home and play with my dogs and spend time with Robson.

The only way I knew to get through the difficult hours at school was to plan and execute pranks.

One of my teachers wore her hair piled up high and quite tight—a characteristic style of the early '70s. I had learned how to make a paper rocket with a sharp point in the front, and I was quite accurate at throwing it wherever I wanted it to land. One day, as the teacher with the big hair stood at the blackboard with her back to us students, I decided to throw a paper rocket, just to get a laugh.

I planned for my rocket to land on the ground near her before she turned around. But I threw it too high and too hard, and it landed nose first in her hair, sticking straight up out of her head. The flight was so smooth, it didn't make a sound, nor did she feel anything. But when the other students saw the paper rocket sticking out of her hair, they burst into raucous laughter.

When the teacher saw the kids pointing at her head, she reached up, felt the rocket, and took it out. She did not see the humor of the situation. "Who threw this?" she demanded.

Knowing I couldn't blame anyone else, I said, "It was me."

She gave me a one-hour detention after school. But I considered the punishment well worth it for the laughter it brought to break up the monotony of the day.

———◆———

Shortly before I turned thirteen, I was moved to the high school building on the other side of the soccer fields, at the foot of a mountain. The first big change I noticed was that we started every morning with an hour of mandatory prayers using our Siddur, the Hebrew prayer book. The school staff wanted to build in students a commitment to prayer and to Judaism that would hopefully carry into our adult lives.

During this prayer time, we would "lay tefillin." This term refers to the process of using leather straps to fasten small black boxes containing Hebrew parchments around the forearm and on the forehead. We did this as a commemoration of God's deliverance from bondage in Egypt and as a reminder to keep his commandments before us at all times. This was in response to a few Scriptures, mainly Exodus 13:9: "It shall be as a sign to you on your hand and as a memorial between your eyes, that the Lord's law may be in your mouth; for with a strong hand the Lord has brought you out of Egypt."

We said the same prayers in Hebrew every morning. At the beginning of each month, based on the Hebrew lunar calendar, we also observed Rosh Chodesh, and said the prayers for the first day of a new month, based on the full moon.

Doing repetitive prayers hundreds of times got boring. So we boys found creative ways to amuse ourselves.

Once, while we were supposed to be engrossed in prayer, one of my classmates tied the shoelaces of the boy in front him together. When the kid stood up, he came crashing to the ground, arms flailing wildly and chairs flying everywhere, all to the tremendous amusement of the spectators.

Another time, a student stealthily grasped the long leather strap that hung from the headpiece of the boy in front of him and tied it to the top of his plastic chair. When the portion of the service came where we were required to rise for prayer, the unsuspecting victim stood, and his chair and all the chairs connected to it crashed, noisily disrupting the solemn moment.

Our teachers chided the guys who had perpetrated these humorous antics. Though I was certainly a prankster myself, I felt it was irreverent to do such things during prayer times. We were supposed to be focusing on God, even if the prayers did seem repetitive, monotonous, and boring. And during these times, in the silent reverence, my mind asked some serious questions.

Does God get even more bored than I do, hearing hundreds of people pray the same things every day? Isn't there a more exciting and interactive way to connect with the Creator of the universe? Since God is obviously way more intelligent than any of us, why doesn't he communicate with his people instead of this "one-way street" of us praying to him? Doesn't he have something he wants to say to us too? Is this all there is to God and to life?

Surely there had to be more.

PASSAGE TO MANHOOD

Turning thirteen is a significant landmark for any Jewish male. The rabbis consider thirteen to be the age of accountability for keeping the commandments of God. That is when a boy becomes a man. This rite of passage is celebrated at a bar mitzvah, which means a "son of the commandments."

On the twenty-second of February 1975, though I'd been studying for my bar mitzvah for almost a year, I felt nervous about standing before the large crowd at my synagogue to chant my portion of the Torah. With trembling knees, I ascended the stairs of the huge wooden bimah. The rabbi gave me the charge.

After singing my portion of the Torah in Hebrew flawlessly, I looked up at him. He nodded, and I could almost detect a small smile on his face.

I don't recall now what he said as he delivered his message. But at the conclusion of his talk, he turned to me and spoke five words I knew I would never forget: "You are now a man!"

Those five words had a profound effect on me. I felt excited, proud, and scared all at the same time. I couldn't be an irresponsible boy anymore; I was now accountable for my actions. The decisions I made would shape my destiny, determining the path I would take and the legacy I would leave.

At that moment, I knew I had to find out what it meant to really be a man.

After synagogue, my large extended family and hundreds of guests gathered under a huge tent my dad had erected in our yard to celebrate. I gave a speech, thanking everyone for their support and for coming to honor my rite of passage. As I spoke, I sensed I was being prepared by the invisible hand of God for a special path that lay before me.

THE BULLY

Though I felt a significant internal change inside me, nothing really changed on the outside. I had the same bus and school routine. And the bullying actually got worse.

A guy who lived a few houses up, David, was one of my worst agitators. He bullied me on the bus and in class, calling me Paffrey instead of Geoffrey. *Paf* was the South African word for wimp. David was a soccer player and quite athletic. When he saw how much his teasing bothered me, he carried on even worse.

One day he phoned me at home and called me names. I couldn't believe he had invaded my only sanctuary.

I told my father I wanted to ride my bicycle to school and back.

"But that's at least ten miles each way," he said with concern.

"I know." I was determined to avoid David and the other bullies.

Dad bought me an Armstrong Flyer, a solid ten-speed racing bike made by a British company called Raleigh. It had dipped handlebars and big narrow racing tires. When I rode that thing in tenth gear on a long, open stretch of road, not even avid cyclists could beat me for speed. Sometimes I went so fast I even overtook the school bus.

One day my father told me that a coworker had said that if I didn't slow down I was going to kill myself in an accident. He passed on the warning, but I never slowed down. I loved the feeling that no one could catch me. I felt free and independent.

I also got really fit from cycling more than a hundred miles a week. Seeing my budding muscles and increased strength made me want more. I filled a huge potato sack with old clothing, hung it by a rope under the oak tree in our backyard, and pounded it till my hands bled. I also joined a gym and began to lift weights. With puberty and testosterone kicking in, David was in for a rude awakening, and my days of being bullied were about to come to an end.

One day in class, the teacher was late, so the students got wild and unruly. David threw a piece of chalk in my direction. It missed me and hit a guy behind me right in the eye. He teared up.

That was the straw that broke the camel's back. I could handle being bullied myself, but I couldn't stand seeing someone who was unable to defend himself get hurt. I'd always had a heart for the underdog.

"David," I said, "did you throw that chalk?" I knew he did, but I wanted to give him the opportunity to admit it.

"No," he said. "It wasn't me."

Rather than call him out on his lie, I said, "You're lucky it wasn't you!"

He stared at me as if he couldn't believe I had just said that. He came right up to my face and looked me in the eye. "What did you say?"

"I said you're lucky it wasn't you."

"And what would you do about it if it was me?"

"I would've hit you," I said matter-of-factly.

"Well, hit me then."

"I don't want to hurt you."

He challenged me a second time, and I responded in the same way. When he dared me to hit him a third time, I snapped. All those months of bullying, of frustration at not fitting in, of wishing my family had never left Durban, all exploded in a single moment. I hit David with a powerful right cross just below his eye on his cheekbone. He went down instantly. I jumped on top of him and pummeled his face.

It took a few of the bigger guys in the class to pull me off of him.

When I finally stopped, the strongest boy in class stared at me like I was crazy. "Why don't you hit me too?" he challenged.

I knew I could beat him as easily as I had David, but I no longer had anything to prove.

No one bullied me at school again after that day. David even tried to make friends with me by asking me to help him with math. He must have been really desperate to ask me that. I was terrible at math.

———◆———

As I grew older, I realized that school wasn't the only place where bullying and fighting prevailed. Johannesburg was a violent city, and many young men got involved with gangs. A gang that protected its members in the event of trouble was called a "backstop," probably because they watched one another's backs. If a kid went to a party and things got out of hand, he could just mention the name of his gang and the other guys would back off if they knew and feared the gang.

All the toughest gangs had cool-sounding abbreviations. The most feared ones were the "Lebs" for Lebanese, "Itis" for Italians, "Chinks" for Chinese, and "Porras" for Portuguese.

I was determined not to play that game. Whenever other students tried to pick a fight with me between classes, I responded without fear. When they asked me who my backstop was, I said, "I *am* the backstop." Apparently everyone thought I was crazy to think I was a one-man gang, so they left me alone.

The problem was, I'd gone from being teased every day to being avoided. I wasn't sure that was much better. But at least no one was bullying me anymore. I was grateful for that.

I did finally make some friends at school. My two closest friends, Amnon Mourad and Nizan Paz, were Israelis. Israeli kids were not socially accepted by the Johannesburg Jews at King David because they were seen as being different. In general, the Israelis were more secular than the South African Jews, almost all of whom were orthodox.

Having come from the Durban culture, I gravitated toward these boys because I too felt like an outsider. Also, the majority of the students at King David excelled in sports or academics or both. Though I was quite muscular and fit at this point, I did not do well at group sports, and I wasn't great in academics either, so I didn't qualify to be part of either of those unspoken elite crowds.

And so … still … I felt like an outsider. I simply didn't seem to fit in anywhere.

5

FOURTEEN, A YEAR OF SHAKING

Many things happened when I was fourteen that really shook me up and dramatically altered the course of my life.

One of the first major turning points occurred during Passover, which coincided with Easter that year, as it often does. As usual, I attended the Rand Easter Show in Johannesburg. I loved this annual event. It was like a state fair, with amusement-park rides, cattle shows, horse-jumping competitions, and companies showing off their new products, such as the latest cars and technology. Of course, there were also vendors from all over the world selling various kinds of food, candy, and drinks. I enjoyed the opportunity to be exposed to other countries and cultures, especially since I had never been overseas.

Though I was not very religiously orthodox in some ways, one thing I refused to do was eat anything with leaven in it during the seven days of Passover.

The Torah requires Jews to eat only unleavened bread for seven days once a year to commemorate our deliverance from Egypt. So every year, we would get rid of all leaven products to make our home kosher for Passover. When I was a child, I went around the house with my mom, carrying a feather and a handkerchief, looking for crumbs, scooping them up with the feather, then throwing them away.

I did creative things to make my diet more interesting that week, including baking matzo balls in the oven and having them with eggs for breakfast. I also put small pieces of matzo in a bowl with cold milk and sugar. It was quite bland, but it was the closest thing I could get to eating cereal without breaking Passover.

Whenever the Rand Easter Show overlapped with Passover, it presented quite a challenge, surrounding me with the aromas of all those delicious foods. But I always managed to enjoy myself without eating anything I shouldn't.

The year I turned fourteen, I was having a blast with my friends, going on rides and visiting the displays. After the roller-coaster ride, I was hungry. In the excitement of the moment, I forgot it was Passover and bought myself a Cornish pasty, which is a flaky pie crust filled with ground beef, mashed potatoes, and green peas. It tasted really yummy after half a day of frenzied activities. I had already wolfed down over half the pie when I realized that this was Passover week … and the pie crust had leaven in it.

Terror struck me. The Old Testament contains 613 commandments, and breaking one is akin to breaking them all. Throughout the Old Testament, I'd read stories about God becoming angry with his people for breaking even the smallest of his commandments. I had just broken an important one. I was convinced that God was furious with me.

For the first time in my life, I had an acute awareness of my sin. And I had no idea what to do to atone for it. For a long time, I could not shake off the guilt of my action.

THE REVOLUTION BEGINS

On June 16, 1976, as I sat in my classroom at school, an announcement came over the loudspeaker. "There have been major riots in Soweto." We all looked out the window and saw plumes of smoke in the distance.

I'd heard that many people in that township had begun marching in protest against the enforcement of Afrikaans as a language of study, as well as against the apartheid system. My understanding was that the protest had been peaceful—until now.

After school, I hurried home to discuss this news with my family. I found my parents in the living room, huddled around the radio with horrified expressions on their faces. I joined them on the couch and listened to the reports about the riots in Soweto.

Apparently, Afrikaans police had thrown tear-gas canisters to disperse the crowds. In the ensuing chaos, many protestors and bystanders were severely injured. Other protestors had been beaten or shot by the police.

The next day, reports of these riots filled the newspapers. During one incident, a curious fourteen-year-old boy came to see what was happening and was shot by a sniper. The image of Hector Pieterson's bleeding and limp body being carried to a hospital, still wearing his school uniform, with his sister weeping uncontrollably by his side, was splashed alongside bold headlines around the world. This iconic image became the rallying symbol of the resistance.

This horror galvanized international resolve to do whatever was necessary to end the injustice of apartheid. Embargoes on South Africa increased. The goal of the boycott was to cripple the economy and thus bring down the apartheid regime. The result was that we felt isolated from the rest of the world.

Strong calls went out to release Nelson Mandela from prison and to unban the African National Congress and groups such as the United Democratic Front and the South African Communist Party. There was an increase in terrorist bomb attacks on restaurants, bus stops, and shopping centers. Haunting images of innocent people maimed and dismembered appeared in the newspaper every day.

Random military roadblocks with sporadic searches became commonplace. Whenever I walked through town or rode in the car with my parents, I saw large military vehicles carrying soldiers armed with semiautomatic rifles heading toward the black townships to quell the riots. I heard people sometimes threw stones at these soldiers—a pathetic weapon, but it was all they had. Their attempts at rebellion were met with bullets. Fatalities increased dramatically, as did the international outcry.

As the struggle took on a more deadly turn, the focus turned to terrorism. Their favorite weapon became the Russia-made AK47 and limpet mines planted at restaurants or other soft targets that would explode and maim or kill those who were at the wrong place at the wrong time. The leaders and organizers of the uprising had been trained and equipped in Russia. Since the apartheid government was paranoid about a Communist takeover, anyone who was anti-apartheid could be labeled as a national threat and imprisoned.

My family and our friends questioned whether we had a future as minority white South Africans. We feared that our country would end up like Angola or Mozambique, where many Portuguese white Africans had to leave their homes in fear, fleeing with only the clothes on their backs, after they were decolonized from Portugal.

The term "white flight" became common in South Africa as many whites, especially educated professionals, began emigrating to more peaceful, established Western nations, such as the US, Australia, the UK, and Canada. This was especially prevalent in Jewish circles, where the citizens tended to be doctors, dentists, lawyers, and such. At home and in school, most conversations centered around which Jewish family was leaving, when they planned to go, and what country they were headed for.

I felt as if the ground were being pulled out from under my feet.

Nothing was certain anymore, including my personal future. I didn't even have a country of my own. I was part of a Jewish minority in an Afrikaans-dominated culture, but I was also part of a white minority in South Africa. Even though the Jewish community as a whole was anti-apartheid, those who were in the uprising against the government saw us as white. As a result, I had to stay away from certain areas, especially the black townships, where I could be killed just because I was white, regardless of my ideology.

To make matters worse, I'd begun struggling academically. I had an especially difficult time with Hebrew and math. While I had a general grasp on reading and writing Hebrew, many of my contemporaries were already fluent in the language, including my older sister, who was a brilliant student.

I had an excellent grasp on the English language, however, and showed a flair for creative writing. I was also a ravenous reader. I often finished books of more than two hundred pages in a day or two. As a youngster, I'd loved British children's author Enid Blyton, and I read many of her books, including her famous Faraway Tree series. As I grew older I read the Hardy Boys detective novels. By age fourteen I'd read many of the famous classic writers. I'd also devoured almost every book written by Willard Price, who wrote books about two teenage brothers who traveled around the world to capture rare animals with their dad, with the aim of preserving them from extinction. Their trips to exotic places like the Amazon to capture rare species and fight evil poachers and opportunists resonated with my sense of adventure and my love for nature and wildlife.

I did fairly well in history class because I found the subject fascinating. I also enjoyed staying on top of the latest trends, different cultures, and international news and events.

My family thought I would make a great lawyer someday since it seemed I could out-debate almost anyone on any subject. Though

I was not very academic, I was quite eloquent. I wondered if I'd find my niche with a future career in law.

THE SHAKING CONTINUES

When I turned fifteen and entered the equivalent of tenth grade, my grades got worse. I did passably well in English, geography, and history, but math and science were like a foreign language to me.

I barely scraped through the school year, and I lost all hope for my educational future. I felt claustrophobic in class, and my mind often wandered off to more exciting adventures. Mostly I stared at the small mountain outside the classroom window and dreamed of climbing it.

The teachers' voices became a distant drone, and all I saw were moving lips and talking heads. I tried to appear attentive and interested, but hoped the teacher wouldn't ask me a question in front of the class. I must have mastered the art of looking intelligent, because I was rarely asked any questions. Either that or I looked like a zombie so the teacher felt too sorry for me to put me on the spot.

Since no one talked to me in my classes and the teachers never asked me any questions, I didn't see any point in going every day. So I started playing hooky.

I spent many class periods climbing the mountain near the school. This *kopie*, as it's called in Afrikaans, was more than a thousand feet high and flat on the top. No one else went there. Just me and nature; that's when I was the happiest.

Thinking I might enjoy a career as a game ranger, I joined the Wildlife Society. My first week, I got together with a group of about fifteen other teenage members and camped out in the wild for a week. We slept under the stars in the open, and lit a fire to keep us warm and scare the predators away. We hiked and climbed mountains for about ten hours a day. So much better than being in school!

There'd been rumors of leopard sightings in the area, so we had to stick together, and our guide remained hyper-vigilant. But I loved the thrill of being in the wild, breathing the fresh, clean air. I felt free. I also felt closer to God when I was in nature, even closer than I did in the synagogue. Which made sense to me. After all, wasn't God the Creator of everything?

On our last day, as we were gathering our belongings in preparation for leaving the camp, some vervet monkeys showed up, hoping to get a few bits of food. Our leader had told us never to feed the monkeys. "If you do, they will begin to see humans as a source of food and they could get dangerous."

Of course, teenagers don't always listen to adult instruction. Behind the guide's back, some of the kids threw scraps to the monkeys. As a result, they followed us as we started to leave the camp.

As we took one last hike, our furry friends joined us. We approached a section of the river where there were small boulders we could use to cross over. The river was quite wide and fast flowing, but the rocks were close enough to one another that we could jump from one to the next and make it to the other side, perfectly dry.

Vervet monkeys do not like water, and these guys had become quite familiar with us. So it didn't surprise me when one of them jumped on my shoulders to hitch a ride across the river.

Though I loved animals, especially cute monkeys, I recalled a story about an aunt of mine who'd been attacked by a monkey and it bit off part of her earlobe. Feeling this animal's breath on my neck, far too close to my own ear, I said, as calmly but firmly as I could, "Would someone please get this monkey off my back?"

Of course, no one came to my rescue because they didn't want to get bitten either.

I started jumping up and down, hoping the monkey would fall off. Instead, he let out a high-pitched screaming sound, which I knew from experience meant he was mad.

Convinced this was a warning that my ear was about to get bitten off, I stopped jumping.

It dawned on me how stupid it was for me to think the monkey would fall off just because I jumped around a bit. Monkeys swing from trees all day! I had to find a different strategy to get rid of my furry passenger.

I stood very still, and as calmly as I could, I loosened the Velcro front of my jacket and slowly lowered the zipper. I looked calm on the outside, but my heart was beating so hard it felt like it was in my throat. Fortunately, my little friend seemed blissfully unaware of what I had just done. In one smooth motion, I whipped off my jacket, with the monkey still attached, and tossed it with all the strength and determination of an Olympic athlete throwing a discus.

The monkey, clinging desperately to my jacket, flew about twenty feet through the air, then landed on his back in the river, with my jacket on top of him. He swam across to the opposite bank, totally soaked and no doubt very angry. But at least my ear was still attached to my head!

Once the danger was passed, I had a good laugh with my friends.

(Years later I heard a song by the American rock band Aerosmith called "Monkey on My Back." I was amazed that these musicians had had an experience similar to mine, even though they didn't live in Africa. In my naiveté I had no clue it had anything to do with drugs.)

———— •◆• ————

I started skipping classes more often than I attended. I even took public transportation into the city on a few school days and went to the movies. I loved the thrill of taking a risk and seeing if I could get away with it without being caught.

No one at school seemed to notice I wasn't there. Not even the teachers. That brought me great delight and relief, at first. Then I realized how sad that was.

It also occurred to me that if I was going to graduate from high school, I needed a more structured environment, where the teachers cared whether or not I was there. I had to change schools.

A NEW BEGINNING

I confessed my truancies to my parents and shared my conclusions with them. When they got over their shock and disappointment, they agreed to look at other options for my last two years of high school.

The best alternative appeared to be Damelin College, at the City Center in downtown Johannesburg. That meant I'd have to spend most my time in the concrete jungle. But there was no turning back now. I was about to become a big-city kid, whether I liked it or not.

At King David, almost 100 percent of my interactions had been with Jewish people. But Damelin College was multicultural. There were many Jewish students, and the school was owned by a Jewish man, but there were also Portuguese students and teachers, as well as Italians, Lebanese, Chinese, and many other nationalities. This was a whole new world for me.

Also, for the first time in my life, I did not have to wear a school uniform. Damelin had a dress code, but students could wear jeans with a nice shirt.

I used public transportation to get to school: a big, red, double-decker bus. That meant a really early start to every morning. But the ride was peaceful and uneventful, which gave me a chance to prepare my mind for the day.

The school was strongly structured academically, being specifically designed to prepare students for a university-level education so they could pursue their career of choice. That turned out to be a lifesaver for me. With the more serious accountability system, and teachers who were the best of the best, my grades steadily improved. I made new friends and began to have a normal social life.

I met a Jewish guy named Roy on the bus to school, and we quickly became close friends. He couldn't immediately replace Robson in my heart, but relating to someone my own age was healthy for me. Roy went to Eaton College, another private school downtown.

I also made friends at school with an Italian boy named Marco. He was the first non-Jewish friend of my own age group I'd had since I was seven. Our relationship greatly assisted in my personal development and my ability to engage in the "real world" beyond my limited experience.

In many Jewish communities outside the US, there is a "shtetl mentality." As mentioned earlier, a *Shtetl* is the Yiddish word for a little Jewish village in Europe where the Jews lived for two thousand years after the exile in the first century when the Jewish temple was destroyed by the Romans. My grandparents in Lithuania grew up in such a community.

This mentality helped us to survive and thrive as a people and a nation. On the negative side, however, it made us a clear target for attack and persecution from those who misunderstood or even hated us for being different and separate.

I never particularly enjoyed living in a shtetl, but it was all I knew for most of my life. Exposure to the broader non-Jewish world in my teenage years was God's way of preparing me for the future calling and destiny on my life.

KUNG FU AND AIKIDO

While at Damelin I was determined to develop my self-defense skills. I was not content to simply never be bullied again. I wanted to master the fighting arts.

I discovered a kung fu club in Glenhazel, a mainly Jewish suburb of Johannesburg, and convinced my friend Roy to sign up with me. The instructor and owner of the studio was a Jewish guy named Mickey

Davidov, a fourth-dan black belt in *jeet kune do*, Bruce Lee's adapted form of kung fu. He was an excellent instructor.

He also taught a form of martial arts similar to the modern jujitsu from Brazil, called aikido. The main principle in this style was using your opponent's strength against him. It was developed by the Japanese so that a smaller, lighter-weight person would be able to beat a bigger, stronger one by using technique and skill against brute strength. While I was by no means small for my age, I was living in a culture dominated by Afrikaners, who were often huge and had grown up playing rugby, boxing, and participating in other physical-contact sports. Many of them were anti-Semitic; violently so on occasion. If I wanted to be a good match for them, I had to really up my game.

But I wanted to do more than get really good. I was determined to make sure no one could ever beat me in a fight if I had anything to do with it. I vowed to be the best—nothing less would suffice. That meant having the edge not only in technique but in fitness as well.

Classes were held three nights a week in the evenings, and the studio was eight miles from my house, mostly uphill. I ran to every class. We started with thirty minutes of intense cardio and core exercises, then practiced striking and kicking techniques for about an hour. After each lesson, I jogged back home in the dark.

I learned how to punch using the ground as my base and how to put my whole body weight into every blow. Training in aikido and kung fu helped me a great deal—not just physically, but mentally as well. It increased my confidence level. It also built in me a lifestyle of self-discipline that has never left me.

———•◆•———

In my first aikido wrestling match, I was paired with a huge Afrikaner who worked for the railways. Kobus was like Goliath and I was David.

Since I didn't know how to use a slingshot, this giant had a good chance at winning!

This tournament consisted of a series of three wrestling matches, with no punching or striking allowed. The way to win was to get an opponent in some kind of hold he couldn't get out of. When he surrendered by "tapping out" on the mat, you would release your grip and be declared the winner of that round. Winning two out of three rounds won the match.

Kobus seemed to be made entirely of muscle, even his head and face. As we approached each other on the wrestling mat, my heart pumped hard with adrenalin and survival instinct. But I was determined to bring this Goliath down.

We faced each other on the mat and bowed, as our instructors had taught us do, in traditional Japanese fashion. "*Hajime*," he said, the Japanese instruction to engage in battle.

I charged my opponent like a kamikaze warrior. I bent my knees, then jumped up at his big head, threw my left arm around the back of his neck, curled it around the front, and locked my hands together in a viselike grip. My feet off the ground, I squeezed with all my strength and hoped for the best. It worked. My opponent came tumbling down. Unfortunately, he landed on me! With his neck still in my grasp, I pulled his enormous body over and then under me. When I looked into his face, I saw it turning an unusual shade of blue. He tapped twice with his free hand.

The fight was over. I had defeated Goliath!

Kobus must have thought I was crazy, because he forfeited the match after one round. And he never fought me again.

Roy and I participated in aikido wrestling and kung fu tournaments at this club for three and a half years. He won many fights, but I never lost a single tournament. I mastered the neck lock so perfectly that no one could get out of it once I got them in it.

I learned some valuable things from aikido wrestling that have held me in good stead my whole life. One is the principle of using an opponent's strength against him. Another is the importance of finding my strengths and knowing my weaknesses. But the main lesson I learned is that it is better to be a master at one thing and the best in your field than to be a jack-of-all-trades and a master of none. By focusing on my tailor-designed neck lock, I was able to win every aikido tournament I entered.

Following my first aikido tournament I turned my focus more towards kung fu and was shortly promoted from white belt to yellow. Soon thereafter I discovered there was going to be an open full-contact tournament on a Sunday morning. Open tournament meant there were no weight divisions, and anyone could enter regardless of what level they were at. Participants would wear gloves on their hands but no shoes. All kinds of strikes were allowed, including kicking. The only part of the body that couldn't be hit was the groin area.

I was really good at kicking, especially the side kick. But I was opposed to doing it to people—that, in my opinion, should be reserved for donkeys. The thought of kicking someone in combat seemed uncivilized and ungentlemanly. Still, I was excited about the tournament and felt a rush of adrenaline at the thought of entering it.

The tournament would be supervised by a referee for the safety of the participants. And it would be based on a point system or a technical knockout to determine the winner. There were time limits per round, and whoever won a bout could continue fighting all morning if he kept winning. Unable to resist, I signed up. I talked my friend Roy into registering too.

My turn came pretty quickly, and my first opponent was an

exceptionally good kicker. But I stuck to my standards against kicking a human being. Besides, I believed my punching power and accuracy was good enough that I didn't need to use my legs.

The guy got in a few good kicks to my body, which hurt. But when I moved out of his kicking range, staying just close enough to throw some short body punches, my opponent folded after just three shots.

As the morning went on, I kept winning, usually within the first minute or two. The aggressiveness of my attacks and the power of my punches were too much for my opponents, and they wilted after a few clean blows.

At the end of the morning, only two guys were left standing: me and my best friend, Roy. He was over six feet tall, lean and wiry, and had a punch like a freight train. He won mostly by TKO: technical knockout.

We had to put our friendship aside temporarily for the sake of the tournament. Whoever landed the first punch would win. It was either him or me, and I didn't want to lose.

After the traditional "Hajime," the call to engage, we did our brief bow. Then I went straight inside his range. Before he could land his powerful right, I got in the first punch: a right cross to his jaw. He went down and the match was over.

All I got was a certificate that acknowledged I had won the tournament, but to me, that piece of paper meant I would not let the world push me around ever again, that I could stand on my own two feet and take care of myself in a tough city in a tough country.

Fortunately, my victory didn't affect my friendship with Roy. We both knew it was just a sport.

———•———

After a few months of kung fu classes, I got bored with theory and technique. I wanted to see how this worked in real life. So I bought two pairs of boxing gloves and took them to class. After the day's lesson was over, I asked the other guys if they wanted to spar with me. Several took me up on the offer.

Every time I put on those red Everlast gloves it made me feel more confident and secure. I soon found out that I had a talent for boxing. My skills as a fighter gave me a new identity.

After I'd beaten everyone who would fight me at the club, I ran out of people I could practice my boxing skills on. There were no boxing clubs in the Johannesburg suburbs where I lived. Boxing was not an accepted Jewish sport. Our focus tended to be on academics and more socially accepted sports such as rugby, cricket, soccer, swimming, squash, tennis, and Ping Pong.

I challenged my sparring partners at the kung fu studio to full-on fights. Not many were willing. I was the hardest hitter there and extremely aggressive, so the few opponents I could persuade to fight me didn't last long. They gave up after I landed one or two blows.

So I went to the street outside the local strip mall and asked adult passersby if they wanted to spar with me. Some agreed. After all, I was just a sixteen-year-old. What could I do to them?

I beat everyone who was naive enough to spar with me.

I was finally beginning to enjoy my life. It felt great not being the underdog anymore. In my new world I was the main dog for a change.

I continued training under Mickey for three and a half years. My main frustration was that I only had two gradings in all that time, which merely got me to orange belt. I desperately wanted a black belt.

One of my fellow students, Larry, started attending the club shortly before I did, and he was a black belt. I figured he must have been teacher's pet and that Mickey had graded him separately in private sessions. I had never been a teacher's pet, either at school or in martial arts.

Larry wore the full kung fu uniform to practices, complete with his black belt, parading in front of all the other students and doing all kinds of fancy Bruce Lee moves. I found him very irritating. This well-built, wiry, muscular kid was the last challenge to my supremacy at the club.

One day, I overheard one of the other guys telling Larry how tough I was, and he replied, "Don't worry about Geoff. He's nothing."

I marched right up to him. "So, I'm a nothing, huh? How about we put on the gloves and go for it? Punching only—no kicking. Full power, no holds barred."

"I'd love to," he said with confidence.

His attitude made me even more furious. After being bullied most my life, being treated with such disdain and disregard was more than I could bear.

We donned our gloves.

I hit him with straight, accurate punches in a controlled rage. Left, right, left. He felt the power of every blow. The expression on his face told me he was shocked and then really scared.

He begged me not to knock him out. I found that pathetic. But I was content to let him off the hook. After all, I'd made my point. And I was not going to become a bully myself. I refused to stoop to that level. My father had always told me that bullies only picked on people they believed they could beat up.

So I let Lance go, and he never messed with me again. I felt as if I had unofficially just earned my black belt!

<hr />

The move to Johannesburg really paid off for me. Not only was I building confidence as I excelled in the martial arts, I was also developing a small but strong circle of close friends. It seemed that my life was looking up for the first time.

My transfer to Damelin was paying off academically as well. I responded well to the more structured system and the individual attention given to monitoring each student's progress. I was actually getting a university-level education so I could qualify for my future career.

I was beginning to find my niche.

6

THE WILD YEARS

I soon grew tired of having to take a bus to school and back every day. Though the legal age for getting a driver's license in South Africa was eighteen, I did not want to wait four years to gain my independence from public transportation. So I decided to teach myself how to drive.

Whenever my parents went out in the evenings, I drove Mom's Toyota Corolla down our long driveway and back into the garage, sometimes at rather high speeds. Fortunately, the brakes were good. Once I'd mastered that, I started taking short trips around our neighborhood.

Being a typical teenager addicted to adrenaline, I considered myself a master of the road after a few short months. So I promoted myself to the "Big Leagues" and started using my dad's Mercedes 280S whenever they went out in Mom's car. On some evenings, I picked up a few friends and drove to a long, wide road that was great for speed.

Sometimes one of my friends got his dad's car, and after checking for speed traps, we raced. We took a two-lane road at breakneck speeds, up to 200 kilometers per hour. Of course I refused to lose a race. It was a miracle that we were never caught by the cops or, even worse, had a bad accident.

One of my older cousins, who worked for my father in one of his furniture stores, had a Suzuki GS1100 GL, a large and very powerful motorcycle. It had twenty-four valves and was as fast as lightning. I begged him to teach me how to drive it.

"You need to learn how to drive a car before you try a motorcycle," he said.

I confessed that I'd been driving my parents' cars, making him promise not to tell them.

He finally agreed to let me try his Suzuki. The thing was huge and heavy. The first time I brought it to a stop, it fell sideways onto the ground and I couldn't pick it up. My cousin, however, righted it like it was a bicycle. Not surprising since he was a black belt in judo and had won the South African Super Heavyweight title. After that, I was more careful.

Once I learned how the gears worked and figured out how to use the clutch, throttle, and brakes, I felt like I could conquer the world. I loved the thrill of such incredible power. Soon I could do a quarter of a mile in just over twelve seconds.

One Sunday, I persuaded a Jewish friend of mine from school named Kenny to go riding with me. He hopped on the back of my cousin's chopper and I took him to a narrow road where the speed limit was 50 kilometers per hour. I was going 120 when I saw two traffic cops standing beside their car, and two cables strung across the road that would read my speed as I went over them.

If I got stopped for going way over the limit, I'd also get caught for being an underage driver without a license. That would put me in serious trouble with the police and my dad. So instead of slowing down, I downshifted and opened up the throttle. Second, third, fourth, I raced through the gears as fast as I could go. The huge motor responded instantly as all twenty-four valves kicked in.

After flying past the speed trap, I looked in my rearview mirror and saw the police officers scrambling to their cruiser. By the time they got into the car, I was a speck in the distance!

When I was far enough away to feel comfortable slowing down, I glanced back at Kenny. His huge grin told me he was enjoying the excitement of the day just as much as I was, confident that he was in good hands with an experienced driver.

On the way back to my cousin's house, I was cruising comfortably with Kenny on the back when a 650cc Kawasaki came zipping past me at about 160 kilometers per hour. I couldn't resist the challenge. I downshifted to third, opened up the throttle, went through fourth and fifth gears in full power, and passed that guy like he was standing still. I glanced at the speedometer and saw that I was doing almost 220 kph. (That's over 136 miles per hour.)

When we got close to the dam, a Porsche 911 came flying past us. No way could I let a big, heavy sports car beat me. I took up the challenge. As I began to overtake him, he veered toward my bike. I couldn't believe he would actually try to drive us off the road. I cleared his car just in time, then put as much distance between him and me as I could.

As we neared home base, I stopped at a red light. When it turned green, I put the bike into first gear and decided to accelerate. To my shock, the front wheel lifted off the ground almost two feet! I was sure we were going to flip over backward. I quickly loosened my grip on the throttle. To my relief, the front wheel came back down and I drove on as if nothing had happened.

"That was awesome!" Kenny exclaimed. "I can't believe you popped a wheelie!"

I didn't tell him it was unintentional.

My cousin told me about the Breakfast Run, a motorcycle race held every Sunday on the long highway that led from Sandton to the Hartebeesport Dam. "All the who's who of the motorbike world go to it, usually hundreds of them," he said. "Well-known gangs such as the Hell's Angels are always there, as well as a group called Satan's Slaves."

"And the police don't stop them?" I asked.

"Because of the huge number of bikers, the cops couldn't stop them all, so they don't even try."

I could hardly wait.

After my first visit to this incredible race, I begged my cousin to let me join in.

"You're too young," he argued.

"No one will know my age when I'm wearing a helmet and gear. And my bike ... or rather, yours ... is bigger than most of theirs, so I'll be able to hold my own with the pack, no problem."

Eventually he relented. And Sundays became my favorite day of the week.

One day, when I arrived at my cousin's house to borrow his motorcycle, he told me I couldn't ride it anymore. "Your father found out about your little escapades somehow. He told me never to let you ride my bike again. Not only are you way too young to drive and don't have a license, but your addiction to speed and risk-taking will eventually get you in trouble, if not killed." He shrugged. "Sorry, Geoff."

When I got home, I confronted my father and tried to change his mind, but he would not be dissuaded. "Motorcycles are coffins on wheels," he said. "In my youth, I saw too many of my friends injured or killed on bikes, and I don't want that to happen to you."

I appreciated his concern for me. But I had fallen in love with motorcycles, and I couldn't imagine never riding one again. I also had an addiction to speed; no matter how powerful the engine of the vehicle I drove I would always push it to its maximum output.

A few of my friends had off-road bikes, and I rode them all, from

175cc's to Husqvarna 400cc's. I desperately wanted to buy my own bike, but my father blocked all my attempts. At the time I was upset. But looking back now, I can see that he probably saved my life. Little did I know that God's invisible hand was keeping me from any path that would bring disaster.

Since I couldn't ride my cousin's motorcycle anymore, I went back to driving Dad's car. I liked his Mercedes but wished it had better acceleration. It didn't have a fuel-injection system, so it was slow on the initial pickup. Still, it was a good car and could reach high speeds eventually. I wanted to see how fast it could go on the open road, but I couldn't risk his finding out and stopping me from driving it.

When my sister Tracy turned twelve, we had a huge bat mitzvah reception at our house after the synagogue service to celebrate her coming-of-age. There wasn't enough parking space for all the guests, so Dad parked his Mercedes on the grassy area near the road, in front of the concrete fence that surrounded our property. I saw this as my golden opportunity. No one would notice if I slipped away from the festivities and tested out the car's top speed.

I nonchalantly grabbed my father's keys from the table beside the front door, sneaked outside, jumped into the car, and fired up the engine. I pulled away into the night and drove the familiar Sandton roads, across the double-lane bridge, headed toward the shopping center. To my delight, I got the Mercedes up to 120 kilometers per hour in a busy area.

After about twenty minutes of fun, I turned around to head home. I didn't want anyone to notice that I, or the car, was missing.

As I sped back across the bridge, another vehicle tried to race me. I picked up more speed. At the far end of the bridge, after a stoplight, the road narrowed into a single lane and the speed limit dropped from 80 to 50 kph. I was going well over 120.

As the light turned yellow, I accelerated, going through the intersection just as the light went red. The car racing me sped through the light as well. I maneuvered the turns on the narrower one-lane road, trying to gain some distance between us. But when I saw a slower car in front of me, I had to put on the brakes to avoid an accident. The car racing me was right on my tail.

All of a sudden, red and blue lights flashed in my rearview mirror. They were coming from the car I had been racing. In the dark, I hadn't noticed I'd been racing a cop car. My heart sank.

I pulled over and put my head into my hands on the steering wheel. Not only had I taken my dad's car without his permission, but I had done it on the most important night of my sister's life so far. I hadn't thought through the possible consequences, and now it was too late.

The officer came up to the door and had me roll down the window. "I need you to follow me to the police station, Son."

Seeing no choice, I obeyed.

"Please don't call my dad," I begged when we got to the station. "If he finds out, he'll kill me." I knew that wasn't true because he was such a kind man. He'd only spanked me on a few occasions while I was growing up. But I hoped that if they thought my father was a violent man, they might feel sorry for me and let me off the hook.

No such luck. They called my dad, told him his son was at the police station, and asked him to come pick me up.

A friend of his drove him to the station. Probably because of what I told the police, they let me go home with Dad, figuring that getting beaten within an inch of my life would be punishment enough.

Of course, my dad didn't do that. But the look of disappointment on his face was worse than any physical torture. Not to mention the guilt I felt at having put a damper on my sister's special occasion, just because I wanted a thrill. I felt terrible and repeatedly told both of them how sorry I was.

Sadly, that incident didn't stop me from future illegal car escapades.

FINAL YEAR OF HIGH SCHOOL

As I approached my final exams for Matric (the South African term for twelfth grade), I was almost eighteen, nearly old enough to get a driver's license. But I was too impatient to wait.

When my grandparents on my mother's side went overseas for a few months on a cruise, I took it upon myself to "borrow" their cars. I reasoned that they would not be using them anyway, so I might as well put them to good use. Of course, I didn't bother asking their permission.

My grandmother's car was a big automatic, which was boring to drive and did not look cool at all. I much preferred my grandfather's car: a two-door Italian sports car called a Lancia Fulvia. It had a high-torque five-speed engine, so it could really fly. And it was very cool looking.

My grandparents lived about ten miles from us, in Greenside, so one day I drove Grandpa's car to the Christian church behind our house and parked it in their lot. Having been sternly rebuked by the priest there for shooting birds and frogs with my friend Gary, I felt justified in keeping my temporarily "borrowed" car there. Finally the church with the annoying neon cross had some use in my life.

I got up early in the morning to go to school, but instead of walking to the bus stop, I sneaked to the bottom of our yard, climbed under the fence, got into "my" fancy sports car, started the engine, and drove to Marco's house. After driving to school as if I owned the vehicle, I parked it in the public lot downtown till our classes were over. After dropping Marco off at his house, I parked the car at the church behind my house, then walked back home. As far as anyone else knew, I was catching the bus every day.

I was so good at hiding my actions and acting normal, no one ever found out what I was doing. At the time, I felt like I was getting away with a lot. In retrospect I now recognize the hand of God protecting me so I would have a clean record, which I would need years later.

My dad bought a second-hand Toyota Corolla for my sister Barbie. On many evenings when she was asleep or not around, I took it on joyrides with my friend Roy. Even though I found automatics boring compared to stick shifts, I tore through neighborhoods at high speeds just for the fun of it and to hone my car-handling skills.

One night, I came speeding around a sharp curve, almost on two wheels, and suddenly saw a police car right in front of me. My heart skipped a beat. I couldn't let them catch me again. This time, I wouldn't get away so lightly.

I flattened my foot on the gas pedal and took an immediate right turn. The police car followed right behind me. I turned off the car's lights so they couldn't get the license plate number.

Mustering all the driving skills I'd acquired since the age of fourteen, I turned every corner as fast as I could without wrecking the car and getting myself killed. I had no time to check my rearview mirror, but I fully expected to see red and blue lights flash on behind me at any moment.

I had a few things in my favor. First, it was very dark. With few street lights in this residential neighborhood, the police had difficulty keeping up with me. Second, I knew those roads like the back of my hand, even in the dark, since I'd gone for joyrides in this area quite often. So even without my headlights off, I could navigate seamlessly through the area at high speed.

My heart raced wildly as I sped around the neighborhood, taking every turn I could, hoping to lose the cops. When I made a sharp right, I realized I had driven into a cul-de-sac. I was trapped at a dead end, with no way out.

I turned off the engine and sat in the dark, waiting. I could practically hear my heartbeat in the silence.

I decided my best option was to act ignorant when the police questioned me and pretend I had no clue what they were talking about. After all, since I had turned off the car lights immediately after they began chasing me, they couldn't prove it was me driving recklessly.

I waited in the dark for what seemed like an hour, with no sign of the police. Then I breathed a huge sigh of relief. I'd escaped again, with no consequences. I started to feel like I could get away with anything.

On a few occasions, I borrowed an uncle's pickup truck that he used for his construction company—this time, with permission. He knew I was underage, but he'd been a naughty kid, too, and I guess he figured boys will be boys. I usually invited my friend Marco to ride in the cab with me.

On one long downhill stretch near my uncle's house, I could pick up some serious speed. The descent was followed by a short, steep uphill climb that suddenly flattened out at the top. After a thirty-foot straight stretch, the road ended at a stop sign.

I discovered that if I hit at least 160 kilometers per hour on the downhill stretch, I would gain enough momentum that when I reached the top of the hill and the road straightened out, the truck would keep climbing. It flew silently through the air for about thirty feet, then land just in time for me to lower the gear, slam on the brakes, and come to a screeching, rubber-burning halt before it went through the stop sign and into cross traffic. I felt like I was landing a commercial airplane on a runway. This really appealed to my sense of adventure.

Not wanting to keep this thrill all to myself, Marco and I sometimes allowed a few unsuspecting friends to hop into the open bed of the truck, telling them we were all going to have a blast. We didn't mention the dip at the top and the flying-through-the-air part! The goal was to see how high they would fly without falling out of the truck.

As our victims rose into the air, then thumped back down when the truck hit the earth, Marco and I broke out into raucous laughter. I slammed on the brakes and slid to a stop just in time.

Of course, the guys in the back did not find this stunt as amusing as we did. No one who fell for this stunt wanted to get into a vehicle with me at the wheel again.

Thank God, no one ever flew out of the truck onto the road.

I loved the adrenaline rush of doing naughty and illegal things. I became accustomed to living on a permanent high from the excitement of taking risks. This was my drug, living on the edge of danger. The greater the chance of getting caught, the more I wanted to do it, just to see how much I could get away with.

With all my recklessness and thrill-seeking, it was a miracle I never got anyone hurt or killed. Naturally, I thought my good fortune was the result of my incredible driving skills and fast reflexes. I didn't yet recognize it as the hand of God protecting me from potential disaster that could ruin my life and my future.

When I finally got my license at eighteen, I calmed down in my driving. Now that I was legal, I found it rather boring.

For a few months prior to taking my final exams, I stayed at my grandparents' house. They lived in Greenside, in a large, double-story brick house. It was quiet there, so I could study without distraction. It was also much closer to school, which meant a quick, convenient bus ride.

My mother's parents, Leslie and Fruma Herring, celebrated Shabbat dinners at their house every other Friday, alternating between our house and theirs. Though we had the occasional clash, as all families do, we were very close.

The Herrings served simple Eastern European dishes at our Friday night Shabbat dinners. We started with cold dishes: chopped chicken livers with onions and a hardboiled egg grated on top, and a chopped herring dish. The chicken livers and herring were spread on *kichel*, which were big, sweet, hand-baked crackers sprinkled with sugar. The main course was a simple but tasty hot dish such as roast chicken or an English pot roast. The smell and taste of these foods spoke of family and tradition. It was the one constant that kept us together during our busy lives in Johannesburg.

The whole family sat around the ornate wooden table in their large dining room, covered by a white tablecloth, with the Shabbat candles burning and the delicious challah bread in the center. Sometimes there were as many as ten of us: my parents, my two sisters, my father's mother Jane, her sister Bev and Bev's husband Harry, my two grandparents, and me.

I was able to study successfully at my grandfather's home since there was nothing there to distract me. When I passed my exams with a university-level pass, I was overjoyed. So were my parents, especially in light of my academic struggles over the years.

Since I'd often been told I would make a good lawyer because I could debate and communicate well, I applied to the University of the Witwatersrand, a prestigious non-government-funded university in Johannesburg where I could earn a law degree. To my excitement, I was accepted. It seemed things were looking up for me, and my future was finally getting clearer.

7

ISRAEL AND MY JEWISH ROOTS

My graduation from high school at the end of 1979 made me both excited and a bit nervous. I was about to enter "the real world."

Every year, the South African Zionist Federation sponsored groups of Jews who'd recently graduated high school to go to Israel for a few weeks. Though I'd grown up with Israel as a centerpiece of my heritage, I had never been to the Jewish homeland. My parents signed me up to go on this trip with a group of about thirty Jewish youth from all around South Africa.

The trip included brief stops in London, Amsterdam, and Germany on the way to Israel.

London was very pleasant and required no cultural adjustment for me. When South Africa had been a British Colony, pounds and pence was the currency, and the British king and queen were ours as well, so our cultures were very similar. I was surprised, though, to see a gang of skinheads beating up Pakistanis on the street while store owners nervously shut their doors. I had naively thought that countries that strongly opposed apartheid would be free from their own racial problems and prejudice.

In Amsterdam we visited the house where Anne Frank lived, in which her parents hid a Dutch family during the Holocaust before the Nazis found her and she was taken to Auschwitz, where she died. The journal entries she wrote during that time became the international best seller *Anne Frank: The Diary of a Young Girl.*

Several Dutch people risked their lives to hide Jews during the Holocaust, and many paid the ultimate price. The ten Boom family, for example, saved countless Jewish lives. Corrie ten Boom's father died in prison, and her sister Betty was killed in the Ravensbruck concentration camp. After the war ended, Corrie wrote books and spoke publicly about her family's experiences. Her autobiography, *The Hiding Place,* was published in 1971 and was made into a movie four years later.

Since I had positive feelings about the Dutch people, I greatly enjoyed visiting Amsterdam. It helped that I could understand the language since it was similar to Afrikaans. I loved the atmosphere of the city, with its canals, great food, excellent chocolate, and generally friendly people.

Of course, I could not say the same for the Germany portion of our trip. Unresolved questions about the Holocaust still plagued me, as was true for thousands of Jews around the world. Even though I did not personally live through it, the results of it touched me personally because many of my ancestors in Lithuania had been murdered by the Nazis.

We visited the preserved remains of Dachau, a concentration camp about ten miles outside of Munich. The purpose for this trip was to cement in our hearts the importance of our Jewish identity and to solidify our support for the Jewish State of Israel, which was essential for the survival and protection of the Jewish people so another Holocaust would never happen.

Seeing Dachau made a strong impression on me as a seventeen-year-old. It was even more impactful for one of the guys in our group, Rudy, who was the son of a Holocaust survivor. His dad, an electrician by trade, had been deported to Dachau. He was forced to maintain the ovens where the Nazis incinerated thousands of Jews, even many who were not yet dead. If he refused, he would have been gassed or thrown into the ovens himself.

Rudy told us that his father often woke up screaming in the middle of the night, having never forgotten the unspeakable horrors he witnessed, things he could not even talk about. "Human beings, made in the image of God, were never designed to see or to hear such things," he said.

I considered it extremely courageous of Rudy to have come on this trip.

The concentration camp was well preserved. As Rudy stared at the remains of this horrific place, I wondered what was going through his mind. In a twisted act of fate, those ovens had preserved his family. Did seeing them bring some closure and healing for him? Or did it open the gaping wound even further? I didn't ask. Some things are best left unspoken.

We also toured the housing barracks, where seven or eight half-starved Jewish people were piled onto each of the tiny wooden bunk beds that were three of four levels high. When the Allies finally came to liberate the concentration camps, many of the survivors were so hungry they ate too much food too quickly. Their shrunken stomachs exploded and they died on the spot, moments away from freedom.

If the goal of our visit to this place was to remind us why Israel's survival is so important to the Jewish people, it certainly had that effect on me.

The phrase "Never again" was coined after the Holocaust and is one of the mottos of the State of Israel and the Jewish people. Never again should we have to suffer such horrors. Never again would we go down defenseless and unarmed. Never again will we fail to defend our families, our people, and our nation against those who would try to wipe our memory from the face of the earth.

This stark image of the reality of the Holocaust made me proud to be a Jew, knowing how the State of Israel was born out of the ashes, largely by untrained and under-equipped Jews who were survivors of the concentration camps. God had not forsaken us. Even through the worst horror anyone could imagine, he showed himself strong on our behalf.

We flew from Germany to Israel. When I got off the airplane at Ben Gurion airport in Tel Aviv, I felt like I was home, even though I'd never been there. Long ago, God promised this land to Abraham and his descendants. And I was one of those descendants.

My enjoyment of the trip was somewhat dampened by the fact most of the guys in our group seemed completely unmoved by the fact that we were in Israel as Jews for the first time. Their focus was on trying to score with the girls. That got old quickly, and I never really connected with them. But the trip did give me a great love for my homeland. I yearned to come back on my own, or with a close friend, and live there. I wanted to really get to know the people, not just be here as a tourist or a visitor.

I loved the sights, the sounds, and the flavors—especially near the street stands that sold nuts and other tasty treats. One of my favorites was falafel, which consists of ground chickpeas formed into balls and deep-fried; topped with lettuce and other greens, humus, and a spicy chili sauce called *charif* in Hebrew; then drizzled with tahini, a smooth paste made from roasted sesame seeds. I also enjoyed delicious *shuwarmas*, which had shavings of grilled lamb, chicken, turkey, beef, veal, or a mixture of meats, along with slices of tomatoes and cucumber, stuffed into pita bread, which I chose to garnish with a fiery red hot sauce. Yummy!

Even more than the food, I found the people here fascinating. They seemed to always shout at one another yet never get into a fight. I found them brash, sometimes even a bit crude and harsh, yet I loved them.

Someone once told me that people who are born in Israel (called *sabras* in Hebrew) are like the prickly pears that grow on a cactus plant: hard and thorny on the outside but soft on the inside. I preferred that to someone who seemed soft and sweet on the outside but was actually hard inside.

KIBBUTZ AND THE FALSE MESSIAH

One of the things on our trip schedule was to spend a few nights on a kibbutz. A kibbutz is an agricultural community where everyone works the land and shares collectively in the profits, depending on their contributions and how long they've been there. Today some kibbutzim are quite technologically advanced, and some even have their own factories and hotels. But in the formative years of the State of Israel, many kibbutzim cropped up and blossomed as a means of survival. They provided for the needs of the families who worked the land and also provided security for the Jewish immigrants.

The first immigrants worked in the Tel Aviv area, doing the tedious job of draining the swamplands and removing rocks by hand and huge boulders by using crowbars so they could plough and till the soil. This area became some of the most fertile land in the country. The finest citrus products grew there and were eventually exported all around the world. Sometimes marauding Arabs attacked them with knives while they were working and vulnerable. So a few Jews were armed with rifles and assigned guard duty each day to keep the laborers safe.

Our group spent a few nights on a kibbutz and met the Israelis who lived and worked there. As we experienced the communal life, I was amazed at how well this system worked and how close-knit the group of people was. More than six hundred people lived there, yet everything ran like clockwork. They all knew their roles and worked the land together.

One night, as we were eating dinner in the huge mess hall with them, a young British Jew approached our table. He introduced himself and said he was visiting Israel for the first time and planned on staying there for a while. Then he took his tray of food to an empty table and sat there alone. He was a rather unimpressive and anemic-looking individual. A group of us joined him to be friendly and keep him company.

As we talked, he suddenly proclaimed, "I am the Messiah, and I have come to Israel to deliver the Jews and to lead them."

I was rather shocked and vaguely amused by his lofty proclamation. My first thought was that if this guy was the Messiah we are all in trouble. I was certain he couldn't even defeat me in a fight, let alone the enemies of Israel! But he piqued my curiosity. After all, I'd been thinking a lot about the Messiah ever since my father told me that Elijah would come during a Passover Seder one year and announce the coming Messiah at God's appointed time.

I decided to cross-examine this guy. I figured anyone who claimed to be the Messiah had to be willing to take some serious backlash. I started with a simple question. "How did you get to Israel?"

"I came on British Airways," he replied.

"When the Messiah comes, he will arrive on a chariot of fire like the one that took Elijah to heaven. I don't think he'll fly British Airways!"

The guys with me laughed. The self-proclaimed Messiah seemed momentarily shaken and I hoped he would rethink his calling. Then he took his tray and went to sit somewhere else.

Though I didn't take this bizarre character seriously, this encounter increased my hunger to know who the real Messiah would be, and how and when he would deliver Israel. After all, I was sitting on holy ground in the very country where the Scriptures proclaimed the Messiah would one day come to rule and to reign.

MY FAMILY AND ISRAEL

The highlight of the trip for me was our visit to the Sinai desert, which at that time was Israeli territory, captured from Egypt in the Yom Kippur War of 1973. At that time, Syria led a coalition of Arab states to try to destroy Israel, attacking them on the holiest day on the Jewish calendar. The Arabs knew the land would be at a virtual standstill on the Day of Atonement, with most public services shut down and the military running on a skeleton staff. They gained some early victories, but they underestimated the resolve of the Jewish people to defend their homeland. Though it was a long, bloody battle, with many lives lost, Israel won a resounding victory in the end. Israelis claimed much of the Sinai desert to provide a buffer between them and Egypt. They also held the mountainous area of the Golan Heights to prevent Syria from waging another surprise attack in such an advantageous position.

A few decades before that war, my family played a part in the birth of the State of Israel. My mother's aunt, a brilliant woman named Dina, grew up in Kipuskis in Lithuania, the same village my mother's mom, Fruma, grew up in. In 1932, when she heard about Theodore Herzl's Zionist dream of a place where the Jews would not be persecuted, she decided to go to what was then Palestine. She tried to persuade others to join her, but no one had the courage to venture into this desolate land full of uncertainty. So she packed her bags and bravely traveled alone, which was unheard of for a single woman in those days.

After she arrived there, she met a handsome young Jewish man named Kurt Givon, who had left Austria because he had the same dream for a Jewish homeland.

This move saved their lives from the Holocaust, where all of their relatives who hadn't left Europe were murdered.

After they got married, he fought in The War of Independence and she served in a supporting role. After independence was gained, they served in the Israeli Embassy to Japan for fifteen years. They both spoke multiple languages fluently.

My uncle Danny also served in many wars as a pilot in the Israeli air force. He was one of the first El Al pilots, and he flew 747 jumbo jets. A few cousins of mine were born in Israel, and many family members living there have served the nation of Israel faithfully.

The history of the Jewish people, including the miraculous rebirth of the nation of Israel, is something I treasure highly, not only because it is about the Jewish homeland but also because it is part of my personal family history. As I walked in places where my ancestors had lived, places I'd heard about all my life but never seen, I sensed a strong connection to my roots.

THE SINAI DESERT

Our group spent a few nights camping in the desert. We went snorkeling in the Red Sea at Sharm El Sheik. It was an incredible experience, seeing nothing but sand everywhere, then going under the ocean and viewing fish of every color, shape, and size imaginable against the backdrop of breathtaking coral reefs. What an incredible contrast.

Then again, the Middle East is a region full of contradictions. Israel was once a desert and now flourishes with trees and vegetation. After being a barren wilderness for centuries, Israel now exports fruit and food all around the world. In fact, Jaffa oranges grow in a region that used to be uninhabitable swampland. When Israel was still called Palestine and under Ottoman rule, what is now called Tel Aviv was swampland, infested with mosquitoes. The Hula Swamps were considered cursed because they were full of malaria and seemed impossible to drain. Now this area is so fertile it is called "the blessed land."

One night, while we were lying in our sleeping bags under the stars, a lone Bedouin walked toward us, leading a camel. At first I thought I was seeing things. How could anyone travel so concisely in this vast desert wasteland? I could barely find my mom's car in the parking lot after leaving the supermarket, let alone make my way through a desert with no markings and no roads. This man had nothing but the stars for a guide.

He seemed friendly, and through sign language we did some bartering with him. Some of the guys gave him packs of cigarettes in return for bottles of a strong Middle Eastern alcohol called arack. Many of the guys got so wasted they vomited all over the place and could barely wake up the next morning. Fortunately, after a small taste, I knew this drink was not for me.

Following our two-week trip, I returned to Johannesburg with a renewed appreciation for my Jewish identity. I was especially comforted to know that I had a homeland that would embrace me if all else failed. I couldn't wait to come back on my own to more fully discover the land on a personal level.

UNIVERSITY AND LAW

Shortly after I returned home from Israel, I applied to the University of the Witwatersrand in Johannesburg. Though I was only seventeen, my application was accepted.

Because this was a private university, not funded by the government, the apartheid regime had no influence on what they taught and they openly spoke out against the government's repressive laws. As a result, the school was considered controversial. The police kept a close watch on all expressions of views concerning the government on campus so they could immediately crack down on any "subversive" activity. If anyone dared to speak out against the racist apartheid policies, even if it was just through a peaceful protest, the "rebellious" individual faced the possibility of being arrested, beaten, or tortured when the police raided the campus.

Though public protests against the government's repressive measures played some productive role, I believed that if people wanted to bring about real change, they should do it in a productive and constructive way, like my father did by providing equal opportunity for all his thousands of employees, regardless of race or ethnicity. Still, I respected the courage of those who made a public stand and paid a dear price for it.

One day, when some students were peacefully boycotting classes, dozens of policemen arrived with German shepherds. They loaded the protestors into vans, dragging some by their hair or clothes. Those who resisted or struggled had the dogs set on them, or were beaten with batons or with whips called *sjamboks*. This long leather whip, used by the police for floggings, was originally made of rhinoceros hide, and it cut deep into the flesh, drawing a lot of blood.

My younger sister, Trace, participated in a demonstration against the second declaration of the state of emergency, which included many inhumane laws such as ten months of detention without right to trial or access to legal representation. The police showed up and fired tear-gas canisters at the crowd to disperse them. When Trace ran, they chased her. After catching her, they whipped her all over her body with a sjambok, resulting in many painful red welts.

Since a high percentage of the students at Wits were Jewish, I couldn't help but sense anti-Semitic undertones in these unnecessary raids.

In addition to the courses required for pursuing a law degree, I signed up for classes in International Relations and English Literature. Those turned out to be my favorites. I loved reading and studying the great English classics from authors such as Jane Austen, Shakespeare, and

Charles Dickens. I especially enjoyed reading *Faust* and the *Canterbury Tales* in their original English version, though it seemed like they were written in another language.

Heart of Darkness by Joseph Conrad, a book about European colonialism in Africa in the early twentieth century, had a profound effect on me. The main character, Marlow, was working for a Belgian trading company when the Europeans came to Africa to "civilize" the natives of the Congo. Marlow set himself up as a god among the tribe where he settled. He eventually became a ruthless dictator, taking advantage of those simple people in horrible ways, all under the guise of Westernizing the "savages." In the end, Marlow used his veneer of civilization to exploit the African people for his pleasure and benefit. He became a savage himself because he was in an environment where there were no consequences for actions. The removal of external laws led to anarchy and evil.

In the review I wrote on this book, I concluded that when the external restraints and laws of Western civilization are removed and a well-educated individual is put in a position of authority, that person can become even more savage than the ones he came to "enlighten" with Western concepts and even religion.

As a Jew living in apartheid South Africa, this story evoked deep questions in my mind. What happens when the external laws of the land enforce racism, even legal discrimination? Those in authority justified these rules by using religious terms and even quoting the Bible. If blacks were not considered equal today, could the Jews be next? And could that lead to another Holocaust?

It seemed to me that the only way to truly change a person or a society was through internal restraint. And that could not be found in any legal system. This made me question my decision to pursue a career in law.

In my International Relations class, we studied political systems, governments, democracy, and the concepts of Western civilization, such as independent nation states. I learned that the League of Nations, which led to the formation of the United Nations, was initiated to bring about world peace, but had failed miserably. I found the concept of a world government scary yet fascinating.

But like my English literature studies, this class evoked more questions than answers. It provided theories and concepts for ultimate world peace through better political and governmental systems, but no solutions for the deeper issues of the human condition that caused wars and turmoil.

I did well in these two courses because I found them interesting and thought provoking. But my law classes were another issue. When a teacher gave me a thousand-page book of court cases to study and memorize, I froze. The only good purpose I could think of for that huge, heavy book was using it as a barbell.

Since many legal terms are Latin, study of this language was essential for a law degree. I actually found this class somewhat interesting. I liked seeing how so many words evolved from Latin roots.

I passed my non-legal-oriented classes. But during my first law exam, I daydreamed like I did in Durban when I was seven years old. I had to find a new major … or at least a new direction in life.

THE NEW ME

During my time at Wits, I became popular for the first time in my life. The first year, I was voted president of my International Relations class, which was quite an honor. I had never been a leader in anything academic.

I was selective in choosing my friends, but I developed a strong circle of half a dozen guys I hung out with regularly. On the weekends we went to a rough downtown area called Hillbrow to play pool, drink beer, and look for girls.

Because my friends knew I was tough, they sometimes tried to provoke fights when I was with them just so they could see me knock someone out. We'd be walking down the street and they would intentionally bump into a guy just to try to get me into a skirmish with him. This really irritated me. Although I actually enjoyed fighting, and didn't think anyone could beat me, I didn't want to start any unnecessary brawls.

Finally, I told my friends, "If you start a fight and someone attacks you, you're on your own. I won't come to your rescue unless you're attacked unprovoked."

I must have made myself loud and clear, because they stopped trying to pick fights for me.

Since I had developed a good build and carried myself with confidence, I had no problem finding a girlfriend whenever I wanted one. I enjoyed my popularity, and I took full advantage of the "new me."

I began seeing women as a form of amusement. I figured their purpose was to feed my ego and meet my sexual needs. But I behaved like a gentleman with them at all times. Though I was sexually active, it was always consensual. In a male-dominated society such as South Africa, it was common for women to be raped on a date, and this crime was rarely reported to the police. But the women I dated felt safe. They knew I would protect them from guys who might want to take advantage of them, because if anyone touched "my girl" he would have to deal with my wrath.

One day, in the beginning of my second year at Wits, I was sitting in the cafeteria with a few of my guy friends during lunch. A pretty female law student sat with us. She was soft-spoken, delicate, and petite.

When I made some egotistical comment that offended her, she locked her deep blue eyes on mine and said, "If you don't believe in Jesus, you're going to hell!"

I was shocked. Where on earth did that come from? I couldn't imagine what I had done to deserve this threat of eternal damnation, especially from such a sweet, pretty young woman. The random statement had nothing to do with the conversation. We weren't talking about anything of a religious nature. Quite the opposite, in fact. I had probably said something a bit crude.

Because there was no apparent context for her statement, it didn't make sense to me. Was she saying that if I didn't believe in some man I knew nothing about, who lived two thousand years ago, I would go to hell?

Maybe she just wasn't a very skilled conversationalist. She'd certainly make a terrible lawyer if she built no foundation for her cases.

As attractive as she looked, I avoided her after that because I had no idea what she might say to me next.

But I couldn't get her words out of my head. Why would I go to hell? What had I done that was so evil? If there was a hell, how could Jesus save me from such a terrible place?

Since most Christians I'd met were terrible communicators of their faith, I still had no clue what they believed or why.

I recalled being in a car with my dad when I was about fourteen years old and seeing a truck in front of us with two words painted in black on the back: *Jesus saves*. I wondered what that meant. Jesus saves who or what? And why and how? I wished the person who started that sentence had finished it. I concluded that he must have run out of paint so he stopped after just two words.

All I knew about Jesus was that most Christians were angry at Jews for killing him. But if they believed that he died so people could be saved, shouldn't they be glad that we killed him? It was all very confusing.

Though I was 99 percent sure this sweet young law student was wrong, what if she was right? What if I got into some stupid fight and a guy pulled out a gun and shot me? Because I didn't believe in this guy Jesus, would I really go to hell?

I figured I'd better be extra careful until I could find out whether this Jesus guy was for real or not.

REBEKAH

I started dating a lovely Jewish woman who was two years younger than me. Rebekah lived in Glenhazel, a predominantly Jewish suburb of Johannesburg, where I had attended my kung fu classes. She was a dancer and studying to become an optometrist. Her mother was a dance teacher and they had a studio in their home, where she taught.

After dating Rebekah for a few months, I began to feel that she was probably the one I would eventually marry and settle down with.

I became increasingly disinterested in school. But this presented a dilemma for me. If I left the university, I would have to enlist in the army. All white males had to join the army when they graduated from high school and serve for two years, unless they got an exemption from the army while they were earning a university degree.

Since the South African army enforced apartheid and was run by Afrikaners, many of whom hated Jews, that was not a very inviting option. Serving in the Israeli army would be preferable, even though that would require I serve for three years instead of two. At least I believed in their cause and would be fighting to defend my people and my homeland. But that would mean leaving South Africa and going to Israel to fight. Which meant I'd need to end my relationship with Rebekah.

I decided to stay in South Africa and serve my mandatory two years so I could be with the woman I loved. Once I found out what I wanted to do for a living after the army, we could get married and raise a family.

To say that I was dreading the next two years would've been a huge understatement. But love can make people do strange things sometimes.

8

THE ARMY

I was sent to an army base at Heidelberg, a few hours outside Johannesburg, for six months of basic training, starting with six weeks of intense boot camp. This time in my life was tougher than I could possibly have imagined. The entire ordeal was designed to break people down as civilians and rebuild them as soldiers.

Heidelberg was a large base with thousands of troops, but it was primarily an infantry training school with an emphasis on radio communications, including interception of enemy broadcasts. After the six weeks of basic training, we spent the rest of boot camp learning about radio communications, including how to intercept enemy transmissions, and using a machine that deciphered coded messages.

The summer of 1981 when I began my stint in the army was during the height of the Cold War, and we considered Communist USSR to be the enemy. They were aggressively advancing around the world and had been very successful in spreading their ideology on the African continent. In some cases they already had puppet leaders in place.

Right on our border, in what is now known as Mozambique, the president was a man named Samora Machel. He was trained by the USSR and was a strong believer in the Marxist-Leninist ideology. At multiple camps throughout his country, as well as in Zambia and Angola, terrorists were trained to infiltrate South Africa and cause chaos.

Ours was the most strategic country on the continent due to its strong economy and abundant natural resources. It had the largest gold reserves in the world as well as platinum, silver, copper, plutonium, and uranium, which the terrorists needed to develop their nuclear arsenal. South Africa was also a key supply route, as all trade ships had to pass the Port of Cape Town, on the tip of the African continent.

Most of the soldiers from our base were eventually stationed along the porous borders with our neighboring countries of Namibia, Zimbabwe, and Mozambique.

Many Afrikaners hated English South Africans and referred to them as "souties," a derogatory term for the English and British. The twenty Jews in my company all spoke English and had been raised under the British education system, and we did not embrace the Afrikaans mentality and culture. So we were viewed as "souties."

Being Jews made us even more contemptible in their eyes. Because the main mess hall had a lot of unkosher food and pork, we had a separate mess hall and we ate separately from the others.

Every Friday, before sunset, an army truck came and picked up all of us Jewish guys to spend the Sabbath in Johannesburg with ultra-orthodox families in Yeoville. We came back in the same truck Saturday night. On Sunday morning, all the Christians lined up on the parade ground, separated in groups by the denominational affiliations they had. They left in several vehicles to attend churches in or near Heidelberg. The largest group was the Dutch Reformed Church, followed by the Church of England, then the Presbyterians, Methodists, Episcopalians, and Catholics.

The Christians took guard duty while the Jews went to synagogue, and we returned the favor for them on Sundays. That seemed fair. But the Christians didn't think so. They only went to church for a few hours, while we got to go all the way to Johannesburg for over twenty-four hours because we were not allowed to drive on the Sabbath. And in the kosher mess, we ate great-quality meals, including delicious steaks, while the food they were served seemed like slop in comparison.

Many of us used the system to our advantage. Several Jewish soldiers became much more orthodox in the army than we had been before. We ate mostly kosher anyway, but very few of us would refuse to drive on the Sabbath. In fact, I had Rebekah park my car around the corner from the house of the Hasidics who hosted us, where we enjoyed a long Sabbath dinner that included a lot more praying than usual.

After the Sabbath meal, I would sneak out to meet Rebekah where she had parked my car and drive to my house to have sex. I used the Sabbath as an excuse to get away from the army and to be with her.

BOOT CAMP

For the six weeks of boot camp, we slept in huge brown army tents with fourteen guys per tent. Our beds were solid metal frames with a thin foam cushion on top. I shared a tent with Roy, my Jewish friend from Johannesburg. Apart from him, there were mostly Afrikaners and a couple of English South Africans.

In July, which is the middle of winter in Heidelberg, the evening temperature commonly fell below zero. One evening, some of the guys washed their uniforms by hand and hung them out on the tent's supporting wires to dry overnight. The next morning they were frozen solid on the wires.

Red buckets beside the tents were always filled with water in case of a fire. The water froze into a solid block of ice during the night. A far cry from the subtropical Durban winters I had grown up in.

I guessed the officers felt that freezing us was a necessary part of the breaking process.

At 6:00 every morning, we had to make our beds perfectly, dress in our clean and pressed uniforms, shave closely, and then stand in formation beside our beds for inspection. Since I struggled to make my bed exactly right, I set my alarm for 4:00 instead of 5:00, like the rest of the soldiers did. When the commanding officer entered, I stood at attention with my chest fully expanded, trying to look as impressive and soldier-like as I could.

The overall atmosphere at boot camp was one of oppression, darkness, and fear, especially among the new soldiers, most of them fresh out of high school. One guy, who was in great shape physically, jumped off a two-story building and shattered his right leg just to avoid boot camp. He was rushed to the hospital and put in a cast, and the army sued him for damage to government property. In their eyes, they owned us for two years.

It was a crazy time, especially for us Jewish guys, most of whom had lived fairly sheltered lives in the upper-middle-class suburbs of Johannesburg. The anti-Semitism was terrible. All the sergeants and corporals called us "Jood," the Afrikaans word for Jew in a derogatory and demeaning way. We felt singled out for being Jewish, as if we were wearing an invisible yellow star like the Nazis made all Jews wear during the Holocaust.

Although South Africa was officially a bilingual country, speaking both English and Afrikaans according to the government, in the army all the instructions were given in Afrikaans. Learning that language had been mandatory in school, but following orders in a language you haven't grown up with is still difficult.

Whenever we did marching drills on the parade ground, commands were barked out in Afrikaans. I quickly learned that *links draai* means "left turn," *regs draai* means "right turn," and *omkeer* means "turn around." Orders were given fast and we were expected to respond immediately. That created a problem because I did not think in Afrikaans. I had to translate each instruction into English in my mind first. The seconds that took affected my response time.

I hated being in this terrible place. My only goal was to finish the two years of mandatory service without getting in trouble and then marry Rebekah. I couldn't have cared less about rank or promotion. I was there purely for love.

My natural aggression and my steady hands for shooting could have been a tremendous asset to the army if I had served in Israel, but I was determined not to use them to further the cause of the apartheid regime in any way. Even though this was not the path I would have chosen, I had to believe that the invisible hand of destiny was guiding my life.

I had been brought up in a well-educated, civilized, mostly Jewish society, where all my friends were pursuing advanced professional degrees in one field or another. Here, everyone in my unit besides Roy seemed rather simple-minded and ignorant. It wasn't just that they had very little formal education. I knew people who were not academically oriented yet were nice people and productive members of society. But the soldiers around me appeared to be from the bottom of the barrel of the human race, both morally and intellectually, and were extremely racist.

I had never met such unseemly characters, and I had about as much in common with them as a sheep in a pack of wolves. I'd grown up in a predominantly Jewish community, and my best friend, who'd been like a brother to me, was a black man. So this level of anti-Semitism and racism, which seemed to be the norm for them, came as a huge shock to me.

Many of the guys in my unit had not graduated high school because they didn't have the mental aptitude to do so. The fact that I had two years of university education, and had grown up in intelligent-thinking circles, made me somewhat of a freak to them. Being Jewish made me even more of a foreign entity. Roy had a high school diploma, which made him as much of an enigma to them as me.

A few weeks after boot camp started, the officers decided to make an example of a few of us. On a particularly cold day, they randomly chose four soldiers. Three of the four were Jewish, including me. The other eight hundred soldiers were told to stand around us beside a small lake, where the corporals told everyone that we were dirty. As a warning for all the soldiers to always stay clean, the four of us were ordered to strip naked and stand knee high in the freezing water. We had to scrub our bodies using a hard wire brush designed to clean floors until our skin was red and raw. It was the most humiliating thing I had ever experienced—especially because of the not-so-hidden implication.

The worst term I had heard Christians use in South Africa was "dirty Jew," implying we were "unclean." This expression was not used that day, but it was implied without words. They'd put one Gentile in our group so we couldn't say we were being singled out for being Jewish.

ANTI-SEMITISM

Much like at King David High School, everyone here had various gangs for protection. And, like I did in high school, I decided to be my own protection. I knew I could hold my own against the Afrikaners if push came to shove, but if I let them know I could fight, they would make my life hell. They hated both Englishmen and Jews, and I was both.

To them, fighting was fun. They got into bare-fisted punching bouts just for kicks. I did it to survive and for the science and sport of it, in a controlled environment with padded gloves. If I beat up one of them, they would be lining up every day to fight me, until one of them beat me. I didn't plan on giving them that satisfaction. I wasn't about to be some kind of trophy they could add to their list of victims. I was determined not to let on that I knew how to fight, even if that meant getting hurt. Otherwise, I wouldn't survive the six months I had to spend in this madhouse.

I devised a plan to make my day-to-day life more bearable. I decided to make friends with one of the guys and ask him to be my personal bodyguard. Why fight my own battles if I could get someone to fight them for me?

One of my tent mates was a guy named Tokkie, which is the Afrikaans word for a metal door knocker. He was so muscular he could knock a guy unconscious with one punch. Even his head and jaw looked like it was made of muscle. I couldn't help thinking that the only difference between him and the Marvel comic character The Incredible Hulk was that the Hulk was green.

Tokkie got into a fight with another big Afrikaner once. With a single punch he shattered the guy's jaw so completely he had to spend six weeks in the hospital with his jaw wired shut, drinking liquids through a straw until the bones reset. Not the kind of guy anyone wanted to get on the wrong side of. But he would make a great backstop for me.

Tokkie wasn't the brightest crayon in the box, but we communicated in short sentences with monosyllabic words. I observed him closely for a while to see how I could become his friend. When I saw him drink an entire can of sweetened condensed milk in about thirty seconds, I felt confident I'd found the key to his loyalty.

Armed with this information, I tentatively approached him one day and said, "Hi."

He peered at me quizzically, like a gorilla sizing up his potential prey.

"Hey, Tokkie, if I buy you a can of condensed milk once a week, will you protect me?"

His face lit up and he mumbled something back that I understood to be yes.

For the rest of boot camp, he was my loyal friend.

Some huge Afrikaners were just waiting for the chance to beat me up, but Tokkie made it clear that messing with me would be the same as messing with him. And no one wanted to mess with him!

One guy especially had it in for me. His name was Tronk, which is the Afrikaans word for prison. He was a prison warden in his secular job, and he was huge and scary. His eyes were set deep in his face and he never seemed to blink. Two guys always hung around with him. One was even bigger than Tronk and very muscular. The other was smaller, but he was an amateur wrestler, one of the best in his school.

One day the three of them picked on my friend Roy, and I could tell they were about to start beating him up. He had no chance against them, and Tokkie was nowhere in sight. The same righteous indignation rose up in me as when David threw chalk into the eye of the guy behind me when I was at King David. I could handle people trying to bully me, but I could not stand anyone bullying someone who couldn't defend himself. My blood boiled and adrenaline pumped through my body.

Not even caring whether I blew my cover, I marched toward them and stood between them and Roy. I looked them in the eye. "If you want to touch him, you have to go through me first."

They peered at me in shock then looked at one another. To my surprise, they backed off. I figured they must have thought I was so tough I could beat all three of them or that I was so crazy they didn't want to fight me. Either way, I breathed a huge sigh of relief. I was safe, at least for the moment.

Once again, it seemed that someone was looking out for me and disaster was avoided. But from that moment on, I knew Tronk and his gang would be out for revenge. After all, they couldn't let anyone think they were afraid of this Jew.

SERGEANT FROM HELL

The sergeant in charge of our unit, a man named Halgreen, had once been a two-star officer. After hearing several frightening stories about the way he treated his troops, I decided Hellgreen would have been a more appropriate description of him!

During a summer intake, for example, I heard he drove his soldiers hard and long in the searing African sun, without enough water. Three of those men died of heat exhaustion. Halgreen was court-martialed, stripped of his officer's rank, and demoted to sergeant, but he still had basically the same role.

At the hearing he said that if he'd known what would have happened, he wouldn't have pushed the guys so hard. But after he was reinstated as a sergeant, he boasted about it to us. "I killed three soldiers through heat exhaustion," Halgreen repeatedly told us, "and I won't hesitate to do it again if you don't follow my orders to the letter." He seemed to delight in invoking fear in the hearts of his men.

As our unit stood at attention, he screamed at us, "*Weet julle wie is ek?*" That meant "Do you know who I am?" We knew he was asking, "Do you realize who you're dealing with? Do you know my reputation?"

Everyone shouted back in unison, "Sergeant Halgreen."

He cupped his right hand over his ear and screamed more forcefully, "*Ek kan nie hoor nie,*" which means, "I can't hear you!"

Everyone hollered his name even louder.

This exercise was repeated five or six times, until he seemed satisfied we all knew how terrifying he was and how dangerous it would be to not obey him.

I thought this was the most stupid and fruitless thing I'd ever experienced. I wasn't afraid of this guy. He was just another bully abusing his authority, and I had sworn when I was fourteen years old that I would never be bullied by anyone again. So when all the guys bellowed out his name, I lip-synched every time, but decided not to waste any vocal energy. I could tell Halgreen knew what I was doing, but since the other guys were so loud, he couldn't prove it. Like my dad told me, most bullies are cowards, and they can sense fear. They can also sense when there is no fear. This guy knew I neither feared him nor respected him. Therefore, he took it on as his personal project to shatter my will.

I wished I was not in this army. I regretted not having moved to Israel, where I could fight for a cause I believed in. I questioned whether I'd made a mistake, even if it was for love.

One evening, Sergeant Halgreen called me aside privately and looked into my eyes with a crazed expression. "Cohen, do you know who I am?" He asked in English this time, so there could be no doubt I understood.

I knew he wanted to hear terror in my voice, but I refused to give it to him. I could have played along, but I did not want to be a hypocrite. Nor did I wish to give him the awe he seemed to crave.

"Yes," I answered matter-of-factly, as if he had momentarily forgotten his name and I needed to remind him. "You are Sergeant Halgreen."

His face turned red. "What am I supposed I do with you, Cohen?" he asked with a voice of steel. "I've tried everything I know to break you, and I can't do it!"

I could not ignore him. So I answered with as much respect as I could muster. "I'm just a soldier, so I can't tell you what to do with me. You're the sergeant, so you'll have to make that decision."

His eyes filled with hate. The veins in his neck stood out so much, I thought they would explode any second. "If I can't break you," he said between clenched teeth, "I'm going to have to kill you!"

His words chilled me to the core of my being. Having already heard three stories about him killing other soldiers, and wondering how many more times it had happened that nobody officially knew about, I considered my life to be in serious danger from this deranged psychopath.

After almost four years of martial arts training, I believed I could defend myself in any situation using my wits and my strength. But I'd decided long ago that I would never fight a crazy person, because psychos would stop at nothing, even if you beat them once fair and square.

Before I went into the army, my grandfather Leslie bought a switchblade when he was in Italy and gave it to me as a gift. These knives were illegal in South Africa because they were the gangsters' weapon of choice. It was easy to conceal the deadly blade until you pushed the switch; then it snapped out, and the sharp point would draw blood if it so much as pricked your finger.

After my personal encounter with Sergeant Lunatic, I decided to get my switchblade from home next time I was on leave and carry it with me at all times. If this madman attacked me when I was alone, I would have no choice but to push the knife right through his belly to save my own life.

I kept that switchblade on me at all times, though I hoped I never had to use it. I didn't want to go to prison for stabbing a deranged sergeant, even if it was in self-defense. I was not confident the military would rule in my favor if I was carrying an illegal concealed weapon.

After a few days of this paranoia, I asked my corporal if I could talk to the captain over our unit.

"What do you want to speak to him about?"

"It's a personal issue, sir. But a matter of life and death."

With little hesitation, he granted my request.

The captain was an Afrikaans woman, and she was surprisingly easy to talk to. I told her the whole story and confessed that I genuinely feared for my life. The only thing I didn't mention was that I'd started carrying a switchblade.

She listened without cursing or screaming at me.

"I understand that the sergeant's job is to break down civilians and rebuild them as soldiers," I said. "But threatening to kill someone you don't like is stepping over the boundary." I asked if I could be transferred to another unit so I would no longer be under Sergeant Halgreen's jurisdiction.

"I have heard of this man's reputation," she said. "And I grant your request to immediately be transferred to another sergeant within the same unit."

I breathed a sigh of relief. I could not fathom why they let this guy keep his position, knowing he was likely to take another life sooner or later. But, again, the invisible hand of God was evident in my life. He was preserving me for a special purpose, even though I had no clue at the time what it might be.

For now, I was happy just to survive another day in this crazy place.

9

BOOT CAMP MADNESS

My transfer to the jurisdiction of a different sergeant meant that Halgreen couldn't threaten me anymore. But the overall atmosphere in my new unit wasn't much better.

The corporals screamed at all the soldiers in Afrikaans, using language so vile I could not repeat the words they said even to the most seasoned curser. The oppression that hung over the camp like a dark blanket was nearly tangible. The whole place smelled like death.

There were about twenty other Jewish guys there. Instead of putting us all together in one tent for our safety, we were split up in ones and twos among the rest of the soldiers. This made us vulnerable to attack.

Every morning we had inspection at 6:00. I woke up at 4:00, as I had before, to make my bed look good. The sheets had to be tucked in so tight the sergeant could bounce a coin on them.

When the commanding officer came in, he went through our things and then checked our faces to make sure we were clean shaven. Since I had a bit of a baby face, my skin always looked smooth.

When my turn came on that first day, I expanded my chest, as usual, to look as impressive as I could. The sergeant put his face within half an inch of mine, checking for any sign of stubble. I felt his breath on my skin, but did not flinch. Finally, he moved on without comment.

Next he inspected the only other Jew in the tent, a guy I knew from Johannesburg. Since my friend was almost six-foot-two, the officer nearly had to stand on tiptoe to check his face. Afterward, he opened the metal trunk next to my friend's bunk. Inside he found the military-issued canvas duffel bag stuffed with unwashed army clothes. A definite violation of the rules.

The tension in the tent was palpable. What was he going to do?

The officer grabbed the duffel bag, turned it upside down, and shook out all the dirty laundry onto the floor. Then he took the empty sack, reached up over my friend's head, and pulled the bag halfway down his body, pinning his arms to his sides. Then the sergeant screamed obscenities at him. My friend stood there with that sack over his head, not moving a muscle, for about an hour. It took every ounce of self-control I had not to laugh. Though I felt sorry for him, the visual was one of the funniest things I had ever seen.

My tent mate did not see the humor in it, however. Shortly after this humiliating incident, he took an overdose of painkillers. Miraculously, he didn't die, but he had to be discharged because he became a suicide risk, which was a liability to the army.

I was actually a little jealous. He'd been discharged after less than six weeks and I still had to finish two years. I almost wished I had enough crazy inside me that I'd be thrown out too. But I couldn't fake that.

After my buddy's discharge, I was the only Jew among the fourteen guys in my tent. I felt like I didn't have a friend in the world.

Shortly after this incident, two more of the Jewish guys who'd come in with me attempted suicide. They both took an overdose of tablets, but the medics got to them in time and pumped the poisons out of their stomachs. So they had to stay.

I thought the anti-Semitism might get better after these incidents, based on compassion. But instead it got worse.

THE SHOOTING RANGE

I'd managed to avoid being set up for active duty due to a medical condition that was identified on my army card, called patella malalignment syndrome. Basically, that's a fancy way of saying I was flat-footed. If I ran a lot or lifted heavy objects for an extended period of time, the pressure could do long-term damage to my knee joints.

When I'd jogged or trained for kung fu, I put firm orthopedic insteps into my shoes. That had alleviated the pressure on my knee joints. But when I went into the army, I decided to use this condition to my advantage.

Soldiers on active duty were regularly ordered to shoot at protestors—many of them teenagers or even younger. They shot indiscriminately at a rioting crowd with live ammunition, and whoever the bullets hit would fall, regardless of their color or age. Most were armed only with stones or maybe a Molotov cocktail, a crude bomb made of a glass bottle filled with flammable liquid. Some were simply in the wrong place at the wrong time. I dreaded the thought of being put in a position where I'd be ordered to open fire on an unarmed crowd. My conscience would not let me do a thing like that. But refusing to obey orders would mean I'd be court-martialed.

Being a Cohen, a direct descendant of the high Levitical priesthood, I had always felt I had a holy calling on my life. And I instinctively knew that God did not want me to shed human blood.

In the Old Testament, God decided not let King David build the temple because he had blood on his hands. Though I couldn't explain it, I sensed this applied to me too. I would not allow myself to take innocent lives, especially in a pointless battle that the apartheid government was waging.

The first time a corporal tried to hand me a rifle, I showed him my army card and said, "This says I can't lift heavy objects because of the strain it puts on my knees. And this rifle is a heavy object." A lame excuse to not carry a rifle, but I saw it as the lesser of two evils.

The army must not have wanted to be responsible if I got a permanent injury, because I was never issued my own rifle.

At the firing range, the other guys would shoot live ammunition at targets while I stood on the sidelines at attention, watching. That worked to my advantage. If they realized I had steady hands and was a good shot, I feared they might want to use my skills to assassinate those whom they perceived as a threat to the regime.

I knew exactly what to do with a semi-automatic, and I would have loved to use one, just for the fun of it. But I couldn't let on.

One day, during rifle practice, my new sergeant apparently got fed up with my sitting on the sidelines. He handed me a weapon, then showed me how to aim at the target and pull the trigger. I gave him a feigned look of confusion. He stood behind me with some other officers, waiting to see what I'd do.

I was really curious to experience the firepower of this custom-made South African R1 rifle. I'd heard it could propel a bullet right through a railway track at short range. But I couldn't let on that I was a good shot.

I tensed my index finger on the trigger till it went white, acting as if I were about to pull it, but I wasn't putting any pressure on the trigger at all. I suddenly swung the rifle around until it was pointing at the officers and the corporal. In my most pathetic voice, I said, "Excuse me, but how does this work again? I forgot."

He tackled me quickly and took the rifle out of my hands, convinced that I was about to mow him and all the officers down in a single uncoordinated swoop. They never let me hold a rifle again, and no one was more relieved than me.

Of course, that gave the Afrikaners another reason to hate me. As a Jew, I was already getting better food in the mess and longer times away for the Sabbath. And now I got to sit out on rifle practice! Why should I be any different from anybody else? Did I think I was better than them? Who did I think I was?

FIGHTING TO SURVIVE

One day, one of the Afrikaners in my tent decided to beat me up over what he considered to be my preferential treatment. When he started threatening me, I longed to defend myself, but I couldn't blow my cover. I had several more months to survive here.

As he threw punches at my face, I kept moving out of his range. His hands lowered to his side, and I had a clear shot. If I threw a left hook I could knock him out. But I resisted the temptation. Instead I tossed a fast left jab toward his nose, just to keep him at bay, but I did not put my body into it as I was trained to do.

The punch was merely a glancing blow, but because of the speed, it shaved some of the skin off the top of his nose and he began to bleed.

Another Afrikaner joined the fight. Koos—a solidly built, stocky guy with big, muscular arms—threw a right hook on the side of my eye. A solid shot. Since I didn't lift my hand to block it, I went down.

I ached to flatten Koos once and for all, but I knew if I did, I would get into fighting wars every day. I had to let them think they had gotten the better of me, for now.

The two of them looked at me with satisfaction, no doubt believing they had taught this Jew a lesson.

I had a black eye for a few weeks, and many times I heard those guys whispering to other Afrikaans soldiers that I'd gotten what I deserved. They smiled with gloating satisfaction whenever they saw me.

Despite my sore, bruised eye, I wasn't afraid of them. However, I let them think they'd gotten to me so they'd leave me alone the rest of my time in this horrible place.

I hated those two guys, especially Koos. I swore that I would find him one day after we got out of the army. I'd tell him that I had let him knock me down just so I could survive boot camp, and then I'd give him the beating of his life. I dreamed of seeing the shock on his face when he saw how hard I could punch. After he went to the ground, I would walk away in disgust just to make my point.

Walking around with a black eye was especially humiliating when I went home on leave. In my neighborhood, I was always known as the tough guy. I'd been undefeated in full-contact martial arts, and my whole identity was wrapped up in being invincible. My black eye communicated that someone had gotten the better of me.

Of course, I'd let those guys do this to me, but no one else knew that. And I couldn't tell them the truth.

I felt like crawling into a hole. And my desire for revenge when I got out of the army grew even stronger.

ANTI-SEMITISM INCREASES

I didn't think my situation could get any worse. But it did.

One day, as a platoon of soldiers was marching, I noticed they were singing a song in Afrikaans in time with their footsteps. The few words I caught sent chills down my spine. One repeated refrain was "*N vet ou Jood van Roodepoort, hy skop die Jood en hy vat die noot.*" The English translation: "A fat old Jew from Roodepoort, he kicked the Jew and grabbed the note." These lyrics spoke about a stereotypical Jewish moneylender whom someone was kicking and beating up. Everyone in the ranks knew the words flawlessly, which told me they were either taught the song in the army or they'd all sung it as kids. And the corporals approved of this, as if it were a normal part of drilling the soldiers.

I feared for my personal safety and the lives of the other Jewish soldiers in that camp. What was to stop these men from killing a few of us if they wanted to? I felt like I was stuck in a Nazi regime with no way of getting out of it. I couldn't refuse to serve or I'd be put in jail.

I heard that some Jewish guys on other army bases had gotten beat up to the point of having to get surgery and even facial reconstruction. If I was attacked, I would be greatly outnumbered. If I ended up injuring someone in self-defense, that would just add fuel to the fire.

All my life I'd wondered if I was a Jew first or a South African first. Now I knew. The decision had been made for me. I was a Jew first … and last.

The hatred and resentment of my tentmates increased until it became almost unbearable to live in the same tent with them. I even heard rumors that the Christians in camp were planning to beat up all the Jews, one by one. I felt vulnerable and at risk for my personal safety. Tokkie was a great bodyguard, but he could not stand against a whole tent of fourteen guys.

I made up my mind to leave this anti-Semitic country and never come back.

I called my father on a pay phone. "I'm going to leave South Africa and go to Israel and serve in that army. At least there I'll be with my own people and not with a bunch of anti-Semites who hate my guts."

"Son," my dad said, "if you leave the army now, you'll be guilty of desertion. You won't be able to get into the Israeli army if you leave this one before your service is up."

I hadn't thought about that.

I told him about the conditions there and how I feared for my life. "If things don't improve soon, I'm going to leave anyway, for my own safety."

"Let me see what I can do," he pleaded. "In the meantime, hang in there and try to lay low."

"I'll do my best, Dad," I promised.

The next day, while we were getting ready to go for breakfast after inspection, a military Jeep arrived in our camp, driven by the sergeant major of our base.

"Signalman Cohen," he commanded, "get in the Jeep!"

I was terrified. What was going to happen to me now? But I had no choice. I jumped on.

He took me to the other side of the base, to the headquarters where the officers lived and worked. I couldn't imagine why I was there. I hoped I was going to be discharged on the grounds that I was of absolutely no benefit to the army. Could there be an award for the "most useless soldier in the camp"? Probably not. Maybe I could suggest it. Playing dumb had worked out pretty well for me so far.

The sergeant major parked the Jeep and told me he was taking me to see the commandant of the camp. He escorted me to an office full of high-ranking officers from the Intelligence unit. I was the only person in the room with no rank.

The furniture was all made of highly polished wood, and medals, flags, and insignia covered every wall. I felt totally out of place here. But at least I was safe from being physically attacked.

The sergeant major introduced me to the commandant. My life was in this man's hands. A single word from his down-turned lips could determine whether the rest of my two years in the army would be bearable or hell on earth.

I gave him my best standing-at-attention salute. "Commandant," I said sharply.

He looked into my eyes. "I've been hearing rumors of anti-Semitism in the camp. Are they true?"

"Yes, Commandant. Three Jewish soldiers have tried to commit suicide because of it. There are times I fear for my life as well."

I thought I detected a glint of empathy in eyes, as if he were genuinely surprised and sorry to hear this news. "That will be all."

"Thank you, Commandant." I saluted, turned around in my best military fashion, and marched out of his office.

The next day, high-ranking officers and a few sergeants and corporals I'd never seen visited the camp. Our entire unit of more than eight hundred soldiers were gathered together and told to sit on the big grassy slope overlooking the parade ground. Everyone around me whispered among themselves, conjecturing about what was going to happen.

A corporal spoke to us in surprisingly fluent English. "According to the South African constitution, people are free to worship God in any way they choose. We will protect that freedom at any cost. We will not tolerate discrimination against anyone because of his religious beliefs."

The guys from my tent glanced at me. They must have thought I had connections in high places, and that was fine with me!

"It has come to my attention that there has been discrimination here against those who are of the Jewish religion. This will come to an end immediately."

After speaking for several minutes about the issue of freedom of religion, he dismissed the crowd.

I walked away thinking what a strange land of contradictions I lived in. It was okay to discriminate against people because of their race and skin color but not because of their religion.

As we returned to our barracks, I still felt an underlying tension. But it was subdued and simmered below the surface now. I breathed a sigh of relief, satisfied that I didn't have to leave the country for fear of my life after all.

Joseph Conrad, author of *Heart of Darkness*, was right when he said that only the external laws of civilization restrain men from doing evil.[1] I was more convinced than ever that if there were no laws in

1 Joseph Conrad, *Heart of Darkness* (Mineola, NY: Dover Publications, 1990).

South Africa to prevent anti-Semitism, pogroms could happen here too.

My mom had told me that people were basically good, and I had believed her. Now I was beginning to question that worldview. Could it be that people were basically bad and only restrained themselves from doing evil things because they were illegal and the law would punish them? My faith in humanity was being shaken to the core. From what I'd observed, mankind hadn't changed much since the horrors of the Holocaust a mere thirty-six years earlier. What would stop those same atrocities from happening again, given the right circumstances?

As soon as I could, I called my dad to tell him about this dramatic turn of events. "What did you do?" I asked with a grin on my face.

"I just called the commandant and told him about the anti-Semitism in his camp and that my son feared for his safety. I told him in no uncertain terms that if he did not bring this discrimination to an immediate end, I would contact every major media outlet in the nation and it would be in the headlines of all the newspapers the following morning."

The commandant knew this was not an idle threat. My father had the authority and influence to accomplish such a thing. He ran one of the largest retail chains in the nation and had thousands of employees. For two years running, he'd won the Business Personality of the Year award from the Department of Commerce and Industry. Therefore, he was well respected in high circles. The commandant did not want his credibility questioned, especially since South Africa was under great international pressure at the time for being racist toward blacks and Indians. They did not need anti-Semitism added to their résumé!

My dad had saved the day, not only for me but for all the Jews in that camp. It seemed that he had been raised up like Esther in the Bible "for such a time as this" (Esther 4:14). He had used his influence for good. And I was proud to be his son.

I had always believed in honoring my father and mother. It's the only one of the Ten Commandments with a promise: "that it may be well with you and you may live long on the earth" (Ephesians 6:3). I had honored my father by sitting tight and not doing anything drastic. And it seemed my life on earth had just been extended and improved as a direct result.

10

PSALM 22

A Greek South African in our intake by the name of John was put in his own tent because of his religious beliefs. That seemed rather bizarre to me. After all, I had different beliefs from everyone else in my tent, and I didn't get a place all to myself. How did a Greek guy manage to get such a privilege?

I asked around and discovered that he was a semi-conscientious objector. Not enough of one to put him in prison, but enough that they feared him being a negative influence and bringing down the morale of the troops. None of the other soldiers were allowed to talk to him.

I found the whole situation fascinating. So out of curiosity, in spite of the communication ban, I decided I had to meet this guy. I wanted to see what made him tick and find out what made the officers so wary of him.

I sneaked to his tent at night, after everyone was supposed to be asleep, and ducked inside his huge tent. John sat on the single metal bed. He invited me to join him for a chat.

"Are you sure? I mean, I am a Jew."

"That's okay. I like Jews."

I had never met a non-Jew who admitted that he liked us.

I sat beside him on his bunk. "Nice place." I decided to jump right in with my questions. "How'd you manage a private tent?"

"I refused to carry a rifle on religious grounds."

I'd gotten out of that with my medical excuse. But I'd never heard of anyone using religion.

"I also refused to march with the other soldiers."

"Why would you object to marching?" That seemed harmless enough.

"According to my religion, marching is vanity."

"Seriously?" I couldn't believe he'd gotten away with that. I wished I could say I didn't want to march because I thought it was vain.

"I belong to the Worldwide Church of God, headed up by a guy named Herbert Armstrong. We observe a lot of the Jewish feasts as well as all the Christian holidays."

Christians in South Africa never celebrated Jewish holidays. How could this guy be a Christian and observe our feasts?

"My church is the only true church. All others are wrong because they don't really follow the Bible. They only follow the traditions of men."

That statement struck me as arrogant to the extreme.

"We print a magazine that's available for free in most malls in the country. It's called *The Plain Truth*." He pulled out a copy from under his thin mattress.

I flipped through the pages of the high-quality glossy magazine. Even at a glance, the articles seemed to be well written and professional. I was impressed.

When I started to hand it back to him, John insisted I keep it. "Read the articles when you have a chance. I think you'll like them."

I had no interest in the writings of a bunch of snobby Christians. But I was starting to like John, and I didn't want to offend him. So I kept it.

"I'm into martial arts," I said, wanting to change the subject.

John's eyes lit up. "Me too. In fact, I'm a black belt." He told me about his form of kung fu, which was not the same as mine.

I noticed that his eyes seemed to look in two different directions. I found that quite distracting because I never knew which one to look at when he was talking to me. But I figured that would make him good at kung fu because the guy he was fighting would never know where he was looking.

"Don't you wish you could use some of your fighting skills against the Afrikaners here?" I asked.

"Oh, I'm not afraid of them. I'm not afraid of anyone, officers or soldiers."

I studied his face, looking for signs of false bravado but finding none. This guy really did seem completely unaffected by the horrible conditions around here.

He attributed his lack of fear to his religious beliefs. "The Bible talks a lot about building character. Well, I believe my two years here are a test from God to build perseverance in me."

John went on and on about his church and its teachings. It got quite draining after a while. This guy was way too obsessed for my taste.

"Look," I said, "I appreciate that you let me in to chat. But please stop talking about Jesus. Jews don't believe in him, you know."

He went to his trunk, opened it, and pulled out an English Bible. I noticed the words New International Version on the spine. After returning to the bunk, John opened to a marked page. "Read this." He put the thick book in my lap.

I read the words on the page in front of me. It said:

My God, my God, why have you forsaken me? Why are you so far from saving me, so far from my cries of anguish? My

God, I cry out by day, but you do not answer, by night, but I find no rest.

How often I'd felt that way, especially in this horrible place. I wasn't sure I wanted to read any further, but my eyes were irresistibly drawn back to the page.

Dogs surround me, a pack of villains encircles me; they pierce my hands and my feet. All my bones are on display; people stare and gloat over me. They divide my clothes among them and cast lots for my garment.

This wording rang a bell with me. I'd bought a record of *Jesus Christ Superstar* years ago and had listened to it dozens of times simply because I liked the music. One of the songs contained lyrics about Jesus being on the cross, where they pierced his hands and feet and cast lots for his clothing.

I handed the open book back to John. "I'm sorry, but this is the New Testament. Jews don't believe in the New Testament."

He raised an eyebrow. "Actually, it's Psalm 22. King David wrote it, and it's in the Old Testament."

I took the book back and checked the page. Sure enough, at the top was a heading that said, "For the director of music. To the tune of 'The Doe of the Morning.' A psalm of David."

How could this be? The words of that psalm clearly described someone being crucified. And that someone had to be Jesus because of the detail about casting lots for his garments.

But how could King David have written this? Crucifixion was invented by the Romans nearly seven hundred years after David's time. How could he have known about this form of punishment and described it in such detail?

There had to be a simple explanation. I closed the book and set it on the bunk. "Your Bible was written by Christians who didn't know the original Hebrew at all. They translated that psalm incorrectly just to make it sound like it's talking about Jesus." That seemed like a good explanation to dismiss what I had just read. But I wasn't as convinced as I sounded.

I told John I had to leave before someone missed me. Though he tried to convince me to take his magazine, I told him I couldn't risk getting caught with it. "It would be proof that I talked to you, and that'd get me into a lot of trouble."

He accepted my excuse.

I tried to forget about the unsettling things I'd heard in John's tent. But I couldn't get them out of my mind.

On my next leave, I went to my grandmother's house. She was quite orthodox. She even had in her home a few copies of the Tanach, the version of the Old Testament Jews use because it was authorized by the rabbis and translated by from the original Hebrew. I wanted to see how the Jewish scholars had interpreted that psalm in order to confirm that the English Bible John showed me was a bad translation.

My grandmother eagerly gave me her Tanach when I asked for it. I found Psalm 22 and read it. To my surprise, the wording was nearly identical to the version I'd read in John's tent, with one exception. Where the English Bible said, "They pierce my hands and my feet," the Tanach said, "They like a lion my hands and my feet."

In the Hebrew language, I knew, the word for "pierced" could also be translated "like a lion," depending on where the vowel was in the original manuscript. But why choose the option that is grammatically incorrect and doesn't fit in the context of the rest of the Psalm? "They like a lion his hands and his feet" made no sense at all. What on earth did it even mean?

Either the rabbis who translated it didn't think this was about someone being crucified … or they were trying to hide something.

If the rabbis were convinced that Jesus was not the prophesied Messiah of the Old Testament, why not let the Scriptures speak for themselves instead of altering anything that might sound too much like it could be describing Jesus? As a Jew, the last thing I wanted was to believe in Jesus. But shouldn't the truth be allowed to stand on its own merit?

If the translation of this verse really was a nervous attempt by the rabbis to cover up the original language, I had no choice but to conclude that this passage must indeed be talking about Jesus.

That put me in a dilemma—not only about believing in Jesus, but also about believing in John, a dogmatic and strange individual who actually seemed to like the Jewish people, and all the dogma of his church being the only true one.

THE CRAZY GREEK

While I was still on leave, John called me at home. "I found something in the Bible that's very exciting," he said. "Do you know that Bible prophecy states that the Germans will once again become a powerful people and try to take over the world? And that there will be another holocaust? And the concentration camps in Germany that are now preserved as memorials will once again become operational?"

I couldn't believe what this guy was saying to me. "John, I'm Jewish. Do you expect me to be excited at your theory that there will be another holocaust? I had relatives who were gunned down by the Nazis!"

"I'm sorry. Really. But don't you see the significance of this?" He tried to explain why he was so thrilled about his supposed interpretation of Bible prophecy. But in my book he had just overstepped all acceptable boundaries. How could anyone be excited about concentration camps being resurrected?

I hung up, interrupting him in midsentence.

Even though John was the closest I had ever seen to a Christian who actually loved the Jewish people, all this weirdness was too much for me to bear. Even if Jesus was the promised Messiah, I thought, if this guy's church really is the only true church, and the rest are all wrong as he claimed, I wanted no part of any of it. If being a believer in Jesus meant I'd become as crazy and obsessive as John, count me out!

I determined to have nothing more to do with John from that moment on.

But Psalm 22 was never far from my mind, even though I had no idea what to do with it.

After a few months John was sent to the psychological ward. I heard he just stared at a spot on the wall all day for weeks until they dismissed him from the army. He hadn't even lasted six months of the required two years. If this was supposed to have been a character-building test from God, John must have failed. Since I'd outlasted him in the army, I figured I had more character than he did, even though I wasn't "in the truth," according to him.

Maybe his version of Christianity wasn't the only truth in the universe after all.

I needed truth at this difficult point in my life. That truth seemed to have something to do with Jesus, but it was elusive. There had to be a missing link somewhere. But I had no idea what it could be.

REBEKAH

After going steady with Rebekah for about a year, our relationship was still strong. But I had no idea what my life would be like after the army; specifically, how I would provide for us.

She had a clear direction already. She was studying optometry.

She was very bright in addition to being very pretty. And we got along perfectly. We hadn't had a single argument in the whole year we'd been dating.

We had sex whenever I was on leave as well as on my Sabbath breaks from the army. Since we were going steady, this seemed perfectly normal. I didn't know whether her parents would approve of that part of our relationship. They were more conservative than most people I knew. But my father had always told me that sex before marriage was okay. Before I started dating Rebekah, I brought girlfriends home and we had intimate relations in my room, and both of my parents were always fine with it. In fact, if a young woman did not consent to sex after a few dates, I stopped dating her. I didn't consider a romantic relationship to be complete without sex.

I recalled John telling me once that sex outside of marriage was a sin. I was shocked. When I told my father what he'd said, Dad scoffed at the idea. "That kind of thinking is from the Middle Ages and does not belong in the twentieth century." He'd always been my moral compass, so I took his words to heart.

My grandfather, Leslie Herring, once told me, after he'd had a few whiskeys, "Boy ..." He paused for effect, then continued in his deep, gravelly voice, "Women! You just love them and leave them."

I knew that by *love* he really meant sex.

My diminutive grandmother was sitting next to him. In her strong Eastern European Yiddish accent, Fruma echoed, "*Ja.* You love dem and you leave dem."

This was the extent of my training and instruction in having relationships with the opposite sex.

And yet, at heart, I was a loyal, one-woman man. I remained faithful and committed to whoever I was dating at the time, and I expected the same from her.

But after that stupid comment from John, I started feeling guilty every time Rebekah and I had sex. Stupid guy! Even though he was no longer around, he was trying to ruin my intimate times with Rebekah, which was one of the few pleasures I had left in life.

SHOCKING NEWS

One day, while I was on leave, Rebekah met me at my parents' home with a worried look on her face. "I missed my period," she said as soon as we were alone in my room. "I think I might be pregnant."

We had always been careful. But I knew that one time without contraception was all it took for this to happen.

I had no idea what to think or say. I'd never thought of a baby being a possibility. No one in our circles had out-of-wedlock babies. Most couples who were going steady used protection—usually the woman was on the pill.

"If I'm pregnant, my parents will find out we've been having sex." Rebekah's voice trembled.

I took her in my arms and tried to think of something comforting to say. But no words came to mind.

I went to a doctor's officer with her. The test results came back positive. She was pregnant.

I was at a loss. My father had never told me how to deal with this consequence. Abortion was illegal in South Africa, and there was no way we were going to get a back-street abortion. I couldn't allow anything that would be a danger to Rebekah.

The doctor advised us to get married and have the baby. "You love each other, right?"

"Definitely." I squeezed Rebekah's hand. "But I'm making a pittance of a salary in the army. I'm in no position to provide for her, let alone a child as well."

"What are your plans after the army?" he asked.

"Well …" I hesitated, not because I didn't want to marry Rebekah but because I hadn't really thought much about life after the army. "I'm confident I could find a good job in the retail industry. My dad manages hundreds of stores. Even if I didn't go to work for him, he has lots of contacts. And he could get me into the best management-training program available."

Rebekah looked up at me, her eyes hazy with unshed tears. For the first time, I actually envisioned us getting married and having a life together.

But we still had one obstacle to overcome, and it was a huge one: Rebekah's parents.

Her dad was a huge, stern-looking man. He was an executive with a large television and electrical firm. I had sensed all along that he wasn't exactly crazy about me. He probably suspected we'd been sleeping together. Getting his daughter pregnant would surely be the final nail in my coffin.

After we left the doctor's office, Rebekah drove home to tell her parents the news. To say that her dad did not take it well would be the understatement of the year. He was furious and even forbid us from ever seeing each other again.

In spite of his ban, Rebekah and I met secretly a few times. She said she still loved me and was willing to carry on with me, even get married without her dad's blessing or approval. I felt the same way about her. But marrying her meant marrying her family. I was not willing to raise kids with a father-in-law who hated his daughter's husband. So I told her we had to stop seeing each other to avoid more pain for everyone.

When Rebekah was nearly three months pregnant, her father took her with him on a business trip to the US. The day they returned, Rebekah called and asked me to meet her in a park.

Her face was pale and her eyes rimmed in red.

"What's wrong?" I asked.

She took in a deep, ragged breath. "I'm not pregnant anymore."

"What?   How—"

"My dad had me get an abortion in the US, where it's safe and sanitary. And legal."

I felt sick to my stomach. "But you were three months along. The baby was healthy and well developed. How could your father do such a thing?"

"He insisted it would be the best thing for my long-term future." She collapsed into my arms and sobbed on my shoulder for a long time.

I tried to think of a way that this situation could be resolved. But there wasn't a thing I could do. I had never felt so helpless in my life.

THE BREAKUP

After that, Rebekah's dad started calling me on the phone and threatening me, saying I deserved to be horsewhipped. I wasn't sure what being horsewhipped entailed, but it sounded terrible. He even called me a murderer. I couldn't believe that he had persuaded his daughter to abort a child, without my consent, yet called *me* a murderer!

I could only conclude that he was a tormented man and his conscience was troubling him.

Even though her father had banned us from seeing each other, Rebekah and I met secretly a few times. She said she still loved me and was willing to carry on, even marry me without his blessing and approval.

I wanted it to work out. I still felt the same way about her. But marrying her meant marrying into her family. I wasn't willing to raise kids with a grandfather who hated their dad.

"I'm sorry," I told her. "But we have to stop seeing each other. Going on will just bring both of us more pain."

Breaking up with Rebekah was extremely painful. But if her father could not give us his blessing to get married, then our being together was not to be. "Destiny must have another plan for us," I said, though I had no clue what that could be.

Rebekah and I cried together for a long time, but we finally resigned ourselves to the inevitable. When we parted, I felt as if my heart were being ripped into pieces.

I had thought that her dad's threatening calls would stop after we broke up. But they didn't. I finally told my father about them. "Don't worry, Son. I'll handle it."

The next time her dad called, my father picked up the phone. "If you ever threaten my son again, I will take you to court so fast you won't know what hit you."

The calls stopped, just like that.

I loved my dad. He was there for me in practical ways when I needed him the most.

But when my leave ended and I had to return to my barracks, I was even more miserable than before. Rebekah was the reason I'd stayed in South Africa, and now I was stuck in an army full of Afrikaners and Christians who hated Jews. I had hoped my years in the service would help me find direction for my life. Instead, my whole world came crashing down around me.

11

HEIDELBERG ARMY BASE

When we neared the end of our six weeks of training in boot camp, we started preparing for a final parade, which all the parents and many high-ranking military dignitaries would attend. I was chosen to lead the march of my battalion. I could not make any mistakes.

As we practiced, the corporal shouted orders in Afrikaans. When he called out, "*Links draai*," which means left turn, I didn't translate quickly enough, and out of reflex I turned right. The thirty guys behind me followed my lead, while two other rows followed the commander's instructions and turned left. The result was a total botch-up of the formation, and I was responsible.

The corporal's face turned bright red. He grabbed my arm and shook me, all the while cursing obscenities at me in Afrikaans. I looked at him calmly, which irritated him even more. He kicked me out of the marching drill, not wanting to risk my messing up the final parade.

I was perfectly content to not participate. My family wasn't going to attend anyway. It wasn't like I was doing something they could be proud of. This army was being used to enforce apartheid. Why would they want to come to a parade celebrating that?

I had to stand at attention for hours, watching the drills. I felt as out of place as a desert nomad in New York City.

After the grueling six weeks of basic training finally ended, we were moved out of the tents and into barracks. We would spend the remaining four and a half months of boot camp being equipped in the field of intelligence and radio interceptions.

In the barracks, in addition to presenting ourselves and our beds in perfect condition for daily inspection, we also had to make the floors so clean and polished the commanding officer could see his reflection in them.

The barracks where Tronk and his goons stayed were just before mine. In order to get anywhere from my barracks, or back to my barracks from anywhere, I either had to pass through their building or go a long distance around their building to get to mine. Knowing they had it in for me and were hoping I'd take the shortcut, I always went the long way around. When I got to my barracks, I could see them through the windows. They looked disappointed.

One day, it snowed briefly and everything was slushy. Tired of the insanity, I decided to amuse myself at their expense. I'd play right into their hands, or at least make them think I was.

My plan was to enter their barracks and walk through it to mine, leaving a trail of muddy boot prints all over the floor. They would be enraged, of course. But as soon as they approached me to attack, Tokkie would come in. Seeing his huge frame, they would back off.

After briefing Tokkie on my plan, and giving him a bonus can of sweetened condensed milk, I took the shortcut toward Tronk's barracks, wearing my muddy army boots. A gleeful sense of anticipation filled me, knowing Tokkie was trailing me at a safe distance so they couldn't see him.

As I opened the door to their barracks, I found the three of them together, as usual. Their faces lit up with glee as soon as they noticed me. It was the first time I'd ever seen them look happy. They were clearly delighted that their most despised enemy had walked right into their hands.

A blanket lay beside the door so whoever came in could wipe his boots before tromping on their freshly waxed floor. I stepped around the blanket and nonchalantly walked toward them.

Their glee quickly turned to anger and then fury when they saw the muddy boot prints I left behind on their perfectly waxed floor. They scowled menacingly and began to advance toward me.

This was Tokkie's cue to come to my rescue. But he did not appear.

My heart skipped a beat. What would happen if Tokkie had decided not to fulfill his part of the plan, despite that bonus can of condensed milk I'd given him? I'd be a goner.

I advanced closer and closer to my adversaries, trying to look as nonchalant as possible, and slowing my pace a bit to give Tokkie more time. They approached me menacingly. I saw murder in their eyes. My forehead beaded with sweat, despite the almost freezing temperature.

Suddenly, just in time, Tokkie's huge figure darkened the doorframe. I quietly breathed a sigh of relief. He looked quizzically at my enemies, as if to ask whether they had a problem with us taking a shortcut through their barracks to get out of the cold.

As he crossed the barracks, without a trace of fear on his face, I noticed that his boots were just as muddy as mine. He glared at my adversaries, silently daring them to go for me just so he could have a bit of fun with them. They didn't take the bait.

After that incident, the crazy three hated me even more. I knew they were hoping to catch me alone in a dark corner somewhere. So

I watched my back everywhere I went.

In retrospect, I realized this was a stupid and dangerous way to entertain myself. I could have been badly beaten up if Tokkie hadn't come in when he did. I had to find better and saner ways to pass the time if I was to come out of two years in the army unscathed.

———•———

Other than these few incidents, I managed to finish basic training without much trouble.

But as the six months finally came to an end, and the commandant of the camp announced that he would be posting our orders for military service in various parts of the country, I was terrified. Spending the next eighteen months stuck in some godforsaken place with Afrikaners and Christians I had nothing in common with sounded like a prison sentence to me.

I certainly didn't want to be sent to the north borders of our country, where army patrols kept Soviet-trained terrorists from penetrating our cities and causing mayhem. I'd heard nightmarish stories of how some guys went crazy over there. At one army camp, soldiers allegedly collected the ears of dead terrorists and wore them as a necklace, like a badge of honor, to show who had the most kills. Not my kind of people, to say the least. Reports of suicides and attempted suicides among the soldiers operating on these borders were rampant. They didn't even use pills; they shot themselves with their own rifles.

I apprehensively joined the long line of soldiers approaching the commandant. As each one reached the long wooden desk, he stood at attention, saluted, and listened to his assignment with a blank expression.

I prayed I would be stationed somewhere close to home.

When my turn finally came, I saluted the commandant. He looked at my file and asked a few casual questions. To my surprise, he spoke in English, with a slight British accent. I answered to the best of my ability, my heart pounding as I waited to hear where destiny would lead me.

He seemed relieved to be having a two-sided conversation with someone who could successfully string a whole sentence together instead of the monosyllabic grunts he'd no doubt heard all morning. I had a good feeling about my brief interview.

Finally he looked up at me with a surprisingly warm expression. "You seem like a rather intelligent sort of chap, so I think I'll put you with Intelligence," he said matter-of-factly.

What a stroke of good fortune! The Intelligence headquarters was at Voortekkerhoogte in Pretoria. It was the closest army base to my home, maybe a forty-minute drive away at the fast speed I usually went. I couldn't have asked for a better assignment.

I felt hopeful for the first time in six months.

FINAL EIGHTEEN MONTHS OF ARMY

After reporting to the Intelligence Department, I was taken to a clean barracks with reasonably comfortable-looking bunks.

I was assigned to work as a cryptographer, decoding important communications and manning the radios, which were connected to a hundred-foot white-and-red interception tower. We were a highly visible target for terrorists, and the whole building was reinforced and bomb-proof. It was like living in a cave. But at least I felt safe.

Because of my high-security clearance level, I could come and go as I pleased, as long as I was in the HQ whenever I was assigned to be on duty. I had to be in my barracks, standing by my bed, for inspections, but they weren't very regular. Apart from that I could go home when I wasn't on duty.

As it turned out, I didn't sleep in my barracks even one night during my entire eighteen-month assignment.

I worked the night shift with a Portuguese-speaking soldier who intercepted terrorist communications in Portuguese and translated them into English. I worked every other night and all weekend, from Friday at 4:00 in the afternoon through Monday morning at 8:00, when a fresh shift replaced us. We both caught a few hours of sleep here and there during these long stints, but one of us had to always be on standby for emergency interceptions.

The benefit of this grueling schedule was that every other weekend I had two and a half days off to have fun and relax.

One day, shortly after I started this assignment, terrorists fired a mortar at us. It landed in a field about twenty feet from our building. Fortunately, it never exploded. I sensed that God was once again protecting me for a divine purpose I was not yet aware of.

———•———

My favorite activity when I was on leave was driving my sports car. I'd just bought a brand-new two-door Ford Escort 1600 Sport. It was a stick shift and came with halogen lights, twin carburetors, and excellent suspension. The body was cream colored, with a cool double black stripe around the side. My dad paid half, and I paid the other half with the bar mitzvah money I'd saved since I was thirteen. I also installed the best sound system money could buy, including high-output Pioneer speakers with tweeters and woofers.

Now that I was out of the emergency-survival mode I'd lived in throughout boot camp and training, I decided to use this season to get into the best physical shape of my life.

Roy and I bought twenty-one-foot kayaks. Two or three times a week we went to a local lake and raced laps around it.

I also joined a professional boxing club in Braamfontein, called the YMCA Boxing Academy. I went there a few nights a week when I worked the day shift. This club had produced some world champions, including Welcome Ncita, one of the best boxers in his division. My goal was to be able to hold my own against every fighter in the gym. I knew that was not going to be a walk in the park.

The training was rigorous, but I liked it. After running up hills and through parks, we came back to the gym, where we worked with the medicine ball, did push-ups and sit-ups, punched the heavy bag, and jumped rope, then sparred a few rounds. That routine meant that if my cardio wasn't great, I'd get beaten up when it came time to spar.

Though I'd boxed a lot, using my martial-arts style of fighting, it had always been in unofficial bouts in the kung fu studio or in my garage at home with friends. I'd never encountered fighters of this caliber. The first time I got in the ring to spar, my opponent punched me in the jaw about twenty times during the first round. I quickly learned that my jaw was not a good way to stop a punch!

I had to adjust my fighting style.

The main trainer, Slagter Van Der Merwe, had trained the South African Olympic boxing team before we were banned from the Olympics. *Slagter* was the Afrikaans word for "butcher." His day job was a butcher, and he had huge hands. But he also had a huge heart.

He saw potential in me and took me under his wing, teaching me in the traditional old-school British boxing style.

"You hold your hands too low," he informed me. "You have very little defense. And you haven't developed a decent left hook or jab."

My knockout right cross had held me in good stead up to this point, but that wouldn't suffice against the speed and timing of these more experienced boxers. If I wanted to maintain the brains I had left, I needed to learn fast.

To my surprise, Slagter scheduled me to fight three of the fastest, leanest guys in the gym. Then he shocked me even more.

141

"I want you to fight using only your left hand," he told me. "Keep the other hand behind your back. Your right hand is your knockout weapon, but that's not enough if you want to become a well-rounded fighter."

It was scary enough being put in the ring with guys who were far beyond my level. But being told to avoid using my favorite, most well-developed weapon seemed incredibly risky. I'd have to quickly develop a powerful left jab and hook or I'd get beaten to a pulp.

Over the next few weeks, I sparred only using my left hand for self-defense. Slagter showed me how to keep my opponents at bay by extending my left jab to its full length. This kept me out of punching range, so they couldn't land any blows. It also forced me to develop a great sense of timing, which protected me from a lot of punishment.

When I had mastered this technique, my trainer let me use both hands again. At that point I felt confident that I could knock out any inexperienced fighter in a short span of time and give a more experienced fighter a good run for his money.

More important, no Afrikaner would ever come close to beating me up again, especially if there was anti-Semitism involved.

After a few months of training, Slagter told me he wanted me to fight professionally.

That caught me off guard. In spite of the fact that this was not an amateur boxing club, I'd thought he was training me purely for love of the sport.

I told him I had no interest in professional boxing. My only desire was to be able to defend myself against the anti-Semitic corporals and soldiers I worked with in my Intelligence unit. If any of them ever were crazy enough to throw the first punch, I wanted to be able to beat them to a pulp.

On one occasion, an Afrikaans corporal made an anti-Semitic slur directed at Jews in general. Something inside me snapped. I lifted my hands and clenched my fists, my cheeks hot with rage. "Let's go outside right now and have this out, just you and me, man to man."

When he realized how serious I was, he backed down, much to my relief. Knowing the shape I was in, I was afraid if I started punching I wouldn't be able to stop. I'd been operating on such a hair trigger for so long, I wasn't sure I could have controlled my fury.

My new boss, Sergeant Major Viljoen, had been a boxer in his time. He never called me by name. He just called me Jood. I wasn't sure he even knew my name, or cared whether I had one. To him, I was just "Jew." Of course, there was nothing I could do about it.

Racism was so ingrained into his generation that all people were defined by their ethnicity. You were either a Jood, an Englesman (or the more derogatory word for the English, a *rooinek*), or a soutie. Only if you were Afrikaans did you get called by your real name.

In a strange way I rather liked the old codger. He'd been in so many fights, all of his teeth had been knocked out. I figured his brains must have had a rough go of it, too, so I didn't blame him for the way he acted.

The Afrikaans corporal who was directly over me at Intelligence HQ during the evenings was a guy named Mack. Apparently coincidentally, he was built like a Mack truck. He was about my age and weighed at least three hundred pounds but was no taller than five foot ten. The guy had no neck—his huge head seemed to simply emerge directly from his shoulders.

Mack was like an enormous human bulldog. He'd been a rugby player for his province and was one of the best forwards in his division. I couldn't imagine anyone being able to bring him down once he got hold of the ball.

Mack and I got along pretty well for about six months. Then one day, as I was leaving my day shift, I told him I wouldn't be back for a few days. "It's the Day of Atonement. We'll be fasting and praying and attending synagogue. But I'll see you when I get back."

His eyes widened. "What?" He leered at me as if I had morphed into a caricature of the devil, complete with horns on my head. "Colin, are you a [expletive deleted] Jood?" he asked in Afrikaans.

I was shocked. I'd presumed he knew I was Jewish. But his calling me Colin instead of Cohen, an obviously Jewish name, indicated he thought I was English. Apparently being English was more acceptable than being Jewish.

He'd grown up on a farm in the country, so maybe he never had the "misfortune" of meeting a Jew before. What a revelation that he'd been working with one for six months.

I half expected him to attack me. Though I was in the best physical shape of my life, this guy was huge. If we got into a wrestling match, he could flatten me like a pancake. I had about as much chance of defeating him as Judge Judy would have of beating up Mike Tyson. So I took a step back, hoping to stay out of his range.

If he attacked me, I could probably get in a few fast, hard left jabs, then try to flatten him with a right cross. If I was court-martialed for striking a superior, I could plead self-defense on the grounds of religious discrimination.

Knowing that would stand up in military court, I opted for a fair exchange of insults. "So," I said, "are you a [same expletive deleted] Dutchman?" There was no worse insult than to call an Afrikaner a Dutchman, since they had declared independence from their Dutch ancestors centuries ago and started their own language, culture, and people.

He seemed puzzled that I was not backing down, seeing he weighed about a hundred and fifteen pounds more than I did.

I had no idea what he might have been taught about Jews. So I tried to reason with him. "Mack, we've been friends for almost six months. I'm the same person I've always been."

The perplexed look on his face told me his brain was trying to cope with this apparently disturbing revelation. "[Expletive] Jood," he muttered.

"[Expletive] Dutchman," I replied, matching his derogatory tone.

We went back and forth this way a few times.

Finally, he looked at me thoughtfully. "You know what, Colin?"

I decided not to bother telling him he'd been calling me by the wrong name for the last few months. His accent was so thick, maybe this was just his way of pronouncing Cohen. "What, Mack?"

"You are a good Jew, and I like you!"

I took that as his rather deranged way of giving me a compliment. I was probably the first Jew he'd ever met. I had no idea what "a good Jew" meant in his mind or why he'd deemed me tolerable. Perhaps this was just a coping mechanism he developed on the spur of the moment to come to terms with the fact that he'd been working with a Jew for six months and didn't realize it.

"You know what, Mack?"

"What?"

"You're a good Dutchman and I like you too."

After that, we were the best of friends.

I managed to finish my time at Voortekkerhoogte rather uneventfully. I couldn't wait to get back home to my mostly Jewish, English-speaking world in Johannesburg. The fact that I'd survived two years in the army without losing my sanity seemed like a true gift from God. I figured he must have a purpose for me, because many guys I knew didn't have such a happy conclusion.

The day my two years in the service ended, I had never felt so happy. I had my whole life ahead of me now.

The question was, what was I going to do with it?

12

A NEW SEASON

The day I completed my two years in the army was one of the happiest days of my life. It was time to press ahead into my future. Though I felt sad about ending my relationship with Rebekah, I felt our breakup paved the way for a new beginning for both of us. It seemed that destiny had a different plan from the one I'd had, and I was excited to see what that would be.

I spoke to my father about Slagter Van Der Merwe's suggestion for me to box professionally. Dad was horrified at the thought. "I'm not even happy that you trained with him for as long as you did."

"Why?"

"How can I tell my Jewish friends, whose sons are all doctors and lawyers and dentists, that my son is a professional boxer? What kind of career is that for an intelligent guy like you?"

I had to admit that boxing was not a very stable or predictable vocation. After just a few months of "boxing boot camp," I had beaten almost every opponent I'd faced, either by knockout or on points, but there was no telling how I would rank with professional contenders.

I had only taken up boxing to be able to defend myself against huge Afrikaners like Mack if I needed to. But in the process I discovered I was quite gifted in this area and I loved the sport.

"The answer for your long-term future is more education," Dad said, "and I'm still willing to pay for it."

"I appreciate that. But no way do I want to study in South Africa."

"How about going to college in the US, then?"

I had no interest in any part of the United States except New York. I'd fallen in love with that city after watching a Woody Allen movie called *Manhattan*, so I thought it would be cool to go there. And after two life-sapping years in the army, I wanted to be where the action was and live it up. So I told Dad, "I agree … but only if I can go to college in the Big Apple."

My father paused, as if surprised by my answer. "Do you agree to drop any further dreams of pursuing professional boxing?"

"I do."

He exhaled a sigh of relief.

I had no idea what field of study I might enjoy. But I recalled meeting a guy in Johannesburg who ran a few clothing factories, and he made a very good living. I'd never thought much about this profession and had absolutely no knowledge of it. But the Fashion Institute of Technology in New York had a program in Apparel Production Management, which taught people how to manage and run clothing factories with an engineering emphasis.

I applied to the college and was accepted.

ISRAEL AGAIN

I still had a few months before classes began, but I didn't want to spend another minute in South Africa. I had to get the army memories far behind me and start on my new beginning. I longed to spend some time in a place where I was not a minority, where I would be among my own people and not be called Jood all the time. So I traveled back to Israel with a Jewish friend named Hilton Lang, whom I'd met while we were training in Voortrekkerhoogte.

Hilton and I decided to work as volunteers on a *kibbutz*, a communal settlement in Israel. Volunteers from all around the world worked at kibbutzim for a few months at a time. They usually worked six-hour shifts six days a week, and the rest of the time was their own. Lodging and meals were provided, along with a small salary and coupons to buy basics at the kibbutz supermarket. For youth who had no money to travel but wanted to have a good time for the summer, it was ideal.

We chose a kibbutz outside Tel Aviv called Shefayim. It was a prosperous community on a large swath of beautiful coastline with pristine beaches. The compound also had orange groves, a plastic-bottle-making factory, and a chicken-breeding industry. The kibbutz hotel, which served both international and local Israeli guests, had a half-Olympic-size swimming pool.

I loved being outdoors. But the first place I was assigned to work was the plastic factory, where I had to wear headphones to drown out the loud *bang* every time a soda bottle was completed, which happened hundreds of times every hour. So much for the peace and serenity of kibbutz life. A few more days of this and they'd have to put me in a straitjacket.

I quickly requested a transfer and was sent to the chicken plant. That was even worse! The workers had to wear high boots because the floors were covered in chicken poop. We also had to wear overalls and long yellow plastic gloves. My team's job was to catch the chickens that were running around in this huge warehouse-type building, at least two at a time, pick them up by their feet, and shove them into tiny cages, after which they would be distributed to a slaughterhouse in the city. The cages were so small, the chickens' heads kept popping up before I could close the wire gates. The workers who'd been doing this for years just slammed the gates shut, even if a chicken's head happened to be in the way.

I couldn't bear to see any animal mistreated like that, even during the last few hours of their lives … and even if they were only chickens. So I asked for another transfer. This time I was sent to work in the hotel, cleaning up after tourists in the discotheque. The work was menial, but whenever I was off duty, I had a chance to meet some of the tourists and hang out with my fellow volunteers. A lot of the workers came from Scandinavian countries, and some of the girls were gorgeous.

The prettiest volunteer at the kibbutz, in my opinion, was a nineteen-year-old from Sweden named Katrina. She had blonde hair, blue eyes, a great figure, a winning smile, and a perfect complexion. I wasted no time in introducing myself to her.

After chatting for a while, I discovered she was fluent in English and well educated. And she liked Israel and the Jewish people a lot. More important, she seemed to like me!

A romance quickly ensued between us. The contrast of my dark features and almost-black hair against her Swedish blonde complexion made us a great-looking couple. She was highly intelligent and a great conversationalist. We could talk for hours on almost any subject.

I became extremely possessive of her. Since she was really hot, a lot of the other single male volunteers fancied her too. I made it clear to them that she was my girl and off limits to anyone else. They had figured out that I had a violent streak, so they stayed away from her. I was perfectly content to let them think whatever they wanted.

It felt good being back on my own turf, among my people. I could set the ground rules once again. I was determined to take control of my life after being dictated to for two years.

As I settled into a routine, I began to love the kibbutz life. I actually regretted that I'd agreed to go study in America, especially so soon after getting out of the army.

The downside of kibbutz life was that since everything was shared and salaries were small, there was little chance for any member to own a home or a car. Those who served on permanent staff were given a kibbutz home, but they didn't own it. And because even dining and social activities were done as a group, there wasn't much private life. But it was all done for the benefit of the group. And that made the sacrifices worthwhile.

After a few weeks in this community, the head of the kibbutz offered me a permanent position on their staff, which I could do easily if I made *aliyah*. Under the law of return in the Israeli constitution, any Jewish person from anywhere in the world could immigrate to Israel as his or her homeland and become a citizen. This was a fulfillment of God's promise to Abraham thousands of years ago, when he said, "I will give this land to you and your descendants."

"You're a diligent worker," she told me. "You're sober and clear minded, which I can't say for a lot of the volunteers."

Most of the people who volunteered there short term were not Jewish. Many went on drinking binges and smoked hashish, the most common illegal drug in Israel. As a result, they weren't good, reliable workers. The fact that I was Jewish was an added plus, because I could get my citizenship and working papers quickly and easily.

I found the offer appealing. I liked the idea of staying in Israel a lot more than going straight to college and studying for a degree with almost no chance to recover, mentally and emotionally, from two long and harrowing years in the army.

I was beginning to realize the toll the army had taken on me. Though I was pleasant enough to be around most of the time, I had a hair-trigger temper with the other male workers. My anger could flare up in an instant, so they all kept a wary distance from me. I needed time to recover from all that.

I called my dad and told him of my decision to stay on the kibbutz.

"No son of mine if going to become a *kibbutznik*!"

His response didn't really surprise me. Living permanently on a kibbutz was looked down upon in the South African Jewish community, where education and professionalism were held in high esteem. It was seen as unambitious, even a copout from real life, where everything was not served to you on a platter. But the security of that kind of life really appealed to me.

In spite of my argument, Dad was emphatic that there was no long-term future in this for me. "You should at least get a good degree under your belt so you'll have a career to fall back on, something you could do anywhere in the world."

I had always held the commandment to "honor your father and mother" in high regard. I knew I couldn't be happy staying on the kibbutz without my father's blessing and approval. So I agreed to move to New York and go to college there.

I hated saying good-bye to Katrina, and she was sad to see me go. We decided to stay in touch by mail and exchanged addresses.

It was also difficult for me to give up my desire to make aliyah. But apparently that was not meant to be.

Though it was a hard thing to do at the time, I realize now that whenever I honored my father's wishes, there ended up being a great blessing in store for me.

THE BIG APPLE

When I arrived in New York City, I understood why it was called the Big Apple. Everything was big, especially the buildings. And the place was filled with forbidden fruit like Adam and Eve ate in the garden. But I was determined to take a large bite out of it while I was there.

Once I saw the vitality and nonstop action of the city, I was pleased I'd come.

I moved into the YMHA (Young Men's Hebrew Academy) facility

on Lexington Avenue and Ninety-Sixth Street.

Being Jewish and South African, as well as a wild and adventurous type, seemed quite attractive to American girls. They really liked my accent. My masculinity also appealed to them. Since FIT was a fashion college, about 90 percent of the students were girls. And many of the male students had little or no interest in women. Those odds gave me a vast playing field, which I took full advantage of.

I soaked in my popularity with the girls, not really caring what the guys thought about me. But I did hang out with some guys from South Africa and other parts of the US. We went to bars and enjoyed the nightlife of the city together.

My friends told me that New York was quite violent in certain areas. They cautioned me against hanging out in Times Square, the lower east side, and a few other places that were known for being very rough. Despite their warnings, I went to all those places and loved them. I found the atmosphere calm and pleasant compared to what I'd experienced in South Africa. Even the gangs and the tough guys didn't scare me. They were about half the size of most of the Afrikaners I'd had to deal with in the army.

I concluded that my friends didn't know what violent and dangerous was all about. Here I felt relatively peaceful and safe, with no danger of sudden riots or police and army roadblocks. And because there were a few million Jews here, no one called me Jood. That was a refreshing change.

I met a guy from Zimbabwe named Mike who was pursuing the same major as me. He had big sideburns that looked like Elvis Presley's, which he wore proudly. He'd been a good rugby player back home and was tough. We became good friends and drinking buddies. The two of us could go anywhere in New York and feel safe together.

Mike was a big guy and knew no fear. He worked as a bouncer at a bar opposite FIT. His job was to break up fights, which he did often.

Whenever somebody turned on him after breaking up a fight, he'd simply lift him off his feet by the scruff of his neck like a rag doll until he calmed down. Some of these guys were sons of the Italian mafia, and they didn't take kindly to that treatment. They weren't used to someone who couldn't care less who their fathers were.

One day, when Mike broke up a fight and kicked a couple of mafia sons out of the bar, they shouted at him on their way out the door, "Elvis is dead. And soon you will be too!"

I strongly advised him to leave that job. "It's not worth getting shot for a few bucks a night."

"I'm not scared of them," he argued. But to my relief, he took my advice and quit.

I got together regularly with a group of Jewish South Africans who attended FIT. We hung out together during breaks at the cafeteria. Most of them were from Cape Town, the most beautiful city in South Africa, in my opinion.

The YMHA had a basic gym. Though it wasn't a boxing gym, they did have a punching bag. A Puerto Rican guy who stayed there was a boxer, and we worked out together to keep our skills sharp.

I discovered a lot of similarities between our countries. Boxing was just as popular in Puerto Rico as in South Africa. And his society also had a male-dominated, machismo kind of culture.

His Puerto Rican girlfriend kept hitting on me, which I found awkward. One day, to my surprise, he told me to go for it with her.

"No, thanks," I said.

Welcome to New York City, I thought. *This place sure can be weird!*

———◆———

In spite of FIT's stellar reputation, there were a few student drug pushers on campus. I met one guy from the Midwest who thought he was tough. He had tattoos all over his body, which I guessed made him feel like he looked scary. For some reason, he had it in for me. But I found his taunts amusing and just ignored him. He probably thought I was a pampered white kid from South Africa. He had no idea what I'd been through. Nor could he have known about my background and training in the fighting arts.

One day this guy and I were both at a coed dorm party. I was standing near him, holding a beer, when he suddenly started taunting and provoking me. I figured he'd had too much to drink. Compared to the huge Afrikaners I was used to dealing with, this punk was child's play for me.

I put my beer down. "You sure you want to do this?"

He put up his fists, ready to strike.

I didn't want to make a scene. But since he was about to throw a punch, I hit him first, with a short, sharp left hook to his ribs just above his solar plexus.

No one saw my punch, but the people standing around us noticed that he doubled over in agony on the floor. The crowd was dense, everyone had been drinking, and it happened so quickly that no one had a clue what I'd done. They probably thought he'd had too much to drink. That suited me fine. I didn't want to draw attention to myself.

With great effort and a lot of grimacing, he eventually pulled himself off the floor. Once he got up, he gazed at me in shock.

"Are you sure you still want to fight me?" I asked casually, as if I were bored with the whole scene.

"No way!" He grunted as he held his ribs. I could tell he knew that any fight with me would be a no-win contest for him. After giving me a new look of respect, he walked away.

The next day he asked me where I learned to punch like that. I told him about my fighting training over the years.

"How come you didn't tell me about that before I picked a fight with you?"

"You never asked."

"Think you could teach me to do that?"

I had no interest in training a feisty guy who would abuse the gift if I taught him how to use it. I'd learned my skills for self-defense purposes only and would not pass them on to anyone who had other motives.

My studies at FIT didn't go well at first. I was good at my business courses and the liberal arts classes, but I struggled with the engineering and production aspects of apparel production management. I decided to change my major to Fashion Buying and Merchandising. That worked out much better for me. My grades improved a lot. I discovered I had an aptitude for marketing, probably the result of the retail environment I was raised in.

My social life at FIT was great. Katrina and I wrote to each other regularly. I could tell she was totally committed to our relationship. She was very pretty, but I wasn't ready to settle down with one girl yet. Quite the contrary. Due to my popularity at school, I dated a lot of girls and lived a very promiscuous lifestyle.

For a while I went steady with a girl from Rochester, in upstate New York. Sarah was a happy-go-lucky, pretty, athletic, blue-eyed, all-American girl with a dazzling smile and a great personality. She was lots of fun to be with. But our relationship was based almost entirely on physical chemistry, and deep down I sensed it wouldn't last.

Though I had quite a few flings and one-night stands that year, at heart I was a loyal, one-woman kind of man and hoped for a deep, long-term relationship. I just hadn't met the right girl. I had thought Rachel was "the one" … until we broke up.

For spring break I went to Fort Lauderdale with a group of other students. I wasn't sure what all the hoopla was about, but I quickly discovered that it was basically a week filled with a lot of skin, drinking, and partying. Being the cool guy on campus, everyone expected me to dive in with gusto. But I found the whole scene quite sickening and empty.

As my first year at FIT drew to a close, I missed Israel more than ever. I ached to go back. Despite how great things looked for me on the outside, I yearned for something that would satisfy the emptiness I felt inside. I didn't know what that something could be, but I was determined to keep looking until I found it.

Spending a hot, sticky summer in the concrete jungle did not sound like my idea of fun. So I wrote to Katrina and told her I was returning to Israel and would be staying at the Shefayim kibbutz for the summer, and we should get together. She wrote back saying she couldn't wait to see me. I asked Mike if he wanted to come along. He'd never been to Israel and agreed to go. I could hardly wait.

ISRAEL AGAIN

As soon as Mike and I arrived at Ben Gurion airport in Tel Aviv, we went straight to the Shefayim kibbutz. It was as beautiful as ever. The well-kept lawns were lush and green. Tall palm trees with enormous boughs swayed in the breeze. The beaches stretching along the sparkling Mediterranean were inviting. I even enjoyed eating in the huge mess hall with more than six hundred people at one time. To my surprise, I realized I missed the communal lifestyle.

The Dutch woman who oversaw all the volunteers was really pleased I was back. "I hope you'll stay for good this time," Margaret told me.

I'd always had a soft spot for the Dutch. I knew many of them had helped hide Jews from the Nazis in World War II, and any friend of the Jewish people was a friend of mine. I thought it strange how anti-

Semitism was so ingrained into the Afrikaans culture, yet their Dutch ancestors were just the opposite. I'd found them to be a very tolerant and kind people, the antithesis of what I'd experienced in South Africa.

The volunteer accommodations had three guys to a room, and Mike and I were put with a Jewish guy from the US who was a recovering drug addict. Many recovering addicts and alcoholics came to the kibbutz from around the world, believing that the healthy outdoor lifestyle would help give them a fresh start and free them from their habit.

———•———

I put my bags in my room and then asked if anyone knew where Katrina was. A couple of gals took me to the beautiful Mediterranean beach on the kibbutz property, where I found her lying on a towel in the sand, watching the waves.

She was as pretty as ever. When I called her name and she turned around, a radiant smile lit up her face and her eyes sparkled.

We walked to a grassy area and sat under a palm tree to catch up on the previous year's events.

As I told her about my year, including the many relationships I'd had with girls in college, her smile disappeared. Since I was never good at hiding things, I told her the whole truth, holding back no details.

When I mentioned that I was kind of going steady with Sarah, she gasped in shock. "How could you be going steady with someone else?"

I shrugged. "You're my kibbutz girlfriend. She's my college girlfriend."

Her eyes went wide. "But I thought we were going to get married."

My turn to be shocked. "Katrina, marriage is the furthest thing from my mind. I'm nowhere near ready for a long-term commitment to anyone at this point of my life. College is complex enough for me without having to think about something so permanent right now."

She started crying.

"I'm sorry, Katrina. I had no idea about how seriously you viewed our relationship."

She took a deep breath and dried her tears. "And I had no idea how casually you saw it." She ran off.

I was disappointed that our relationship was over. It had been rather convenient for me to have one girlfriend on each continent I visited. But clearly Katrina didn't like the arrangement as much as I did. Oh, well. There were more fish in the sea, and I was quite happy to keep fishing.

After a few weeks, the Jewish guy moved out of our room to go back to the US, and a guy named Frank came in to take his place. He was from Washington DC and called himself a born-again Christian.

I wasn't quite sure what that meant. But I wondered if he was another nut like John, the Greek guy from the army. He was just as vocal about his faith, which irritated me. I'd come back to Israel to get away from Christians, and now one was living in the same room with me!

Frank was different from most Christians I'd met. He seemed to really love Israel and the Jewish people. But he talked about Jesus almost nonstop. In fact, he spoke about him like he actually knew the guy personally. I found that kind of weird but also quite intriguing.

One day Frank was talking about certain sites in Jerusalem where Jesus had walked that were considered holy to Christians. I'd been to Jerusalem many times, but I always thought of it as a Jewish city, not a Christian one. I didn't even know Jesus had ever been there. I thought he was the first Catholic and the founder of the Catholic faith.

One night, after we all finished our various work assignments, ten of us volunteers sat in a semicircle under the stars on the porch, surrounded by palm trees, drinking cold Israeli Maccabee beer and just chilling. Mike sat on my right, Frank on my left. A British guy named Charles sat across from me.

We began with light, random chatter. Then, as often happens in such settings, the conversation veered toward politics and current events. We spoke about Israel's occupation of Southern Lebanon and whether it had been a good move for them to invade the country in 1982. We discussed communism and capitalism and the aggressive role the Soviets were playing in arming the Arab countries to try to get a foothold in the region. We discussed what we each of us believed was the solution to the crisis in the Middle East.

Of course, with such a diverse crowd, there were numerous opinions, and many people were passionate about their particular views. The conversation got quite heated.

Frank, who'd been quiet during most of the debate, finally chimed in. "The problem isn't communism or capitalism," he declared passionately. "The problem is sin."

Here we go again, I thought. He's about to start preaching. Just what we need, another Christian sermon.

Apparently unmoved by our cynical expressions, Frank continued. "Due to our selfish human nature, we all have a desire to dominate. Each country wants their system to prevail because they believe they have the solution to the world's problems. That's why there are wars. We fight each other so we can enforce our system on others."

His simplistic explanation of sin made a light turn on inside me. Judaism had taught me that all men were basically good. But Frank was saying all men were inherently selfish. Based on my twenty-two years of experience with people, that made a lot of sense to me.

"My father was vice secretary to the US Navy, so I grew up around high political circles. Because of peer pressure, I started taking drugs and became addicted. But when Jesus came into my life, he set me free. You see, Jesus suffered and died on the cross for every human being. Because of his selfless sacrifice, I'm totally free from drugs and addiction. My life is full of meaning and purpose now."

Charles interrupted him. "When Jesus was on the cross, he was doing transcendental meditation at the time. So he didn't actually feel any pain."

What an idiot, I thought. How could anyone think that someone who was nailed to a cross would not feel a lot of pain? Charles's eyes looked bloodshot, as usual. He was obviously high on something.

Frank's face turned bright red and the veins in his thick neck stood out. "You will have to stand before Jesus on the Day of Judgment and tell him that he did not suffer on the cross when he died for your sins!"

Everyone but me argued with Frank. But he clearly didn't care what anyone else thought about what he said. He was fully convinced, and no one was going to persuade him otherwise.

Charles was supposedly a recovering alcoholic, but I had never seen him sober. In fact, most of the time he was so inebriated he couldn't work in any section of the kibbutz for very long. He was totally unreliable. He ended up becoming the driver of the tractor trailer that towed bags of dirty clothes from the kibbutz to the laundry facility across a huge, empty field where there was nothing he could crash into. It was the only job he could do because it was so simple it was almost impossible to mess up, even for him. I'd never taken him seriously.

Frank, on the other hand, had complete conviction about his faith in God and where he was going in life. I really admired his passion. Here was a guy who was willing to put his life on the line for what he believed. Now, that was someone I could respect.

Part of me wanted to talk to Frank about the things he'd just shared. But I was still gun-shy from my bad experience with John the Greek, who had turned out to be so weird. Frank seemed different, and I hoped he was. But I couldn't be sure that he wouldn't turn out to be just as strange as John.

Shortly after that evening, Frank left the kibbutz. But I continued to mull over the things he'd said.

———•———

One Friday night, I went to the discotheque at the kibbutz hotel. Though it felt odd for me to be in Israel and not observe the Sabbath, this was a secular kibbutz, so most Jewish traditions weren't observed religiously there. I met a group of German tourists who worked for a travel agency. They were the top agents in their company and had been rewarded with a free trip to the Holy Land.

I didn't like Germans much, but one young woman from the group caught my eye. She was about twenty and extremely pretty, with a great figure. That was enough for me to overlook the fact that she was German, at least for one night. She was dancing with another guy, so I decided to ask her for the next dance. But when I looked for her after the song ended, she was gone.

I asked a guy from her group about her, and he said she'd gone to her room for the night.

"I really wanted to dance with her. Would you mind telling me which room she's in?"

To my surprise, he told me.

I went to her room and knocked on the door. When she opened it, I introduced myself and asked if she'd mind coming back down to dance with me. She gladly agreed.

We danced and drank for quite a while. Sometime after midnight, we went outside and sat on a bench under the stars, where we talked and kissed. I asked her if she'd like to come to my room with me.

She looked at me with kindness and longing. "I'd love to. But I don't think Jesus would be happy about it if I did."

That was the last thing I expected to hear. I was asking if she wanted to have sex with me, and she started talking about Jesus. What did he have to do with this? Why would someone who died two thousand years ago care whether we had sex or not? I just couldn't connect the dots.

Though I was disappointed and mystified by her strange response, I respected her decision.

When I woke up the next morning and thought about the previous night, I felt an incredible love in my heart. I had to pull myself together. I couldn't fall in love with a German woman! For all I knew her father had been one of the Nazis who murdered my relatives in Lithuania. What was wrong with me?

No matter how hard I tried, I could not shake the feelings I had. But they made absolutely no sense. No way could I fall in love overnight, especially with a German girl. It would take months for me to even be able to trust a German, let alone fall in love with one, no matter how pretty and sweet she might be.

Then where could these feelings be coming from?

I wondered if the incredible love I felt might have something to do with this Jesus she talked about. That made no sense. But this feeling that warmed my heart like a gentle glow was different from any emotion I had ever experienced with a woman.

Was I going crazy? Or was this Jesus following me wherever I went?

13

JERUSALEM

"I love Jerusalem," I told Mike repeatedly. "There's no city like it in the world."

My friend had never been to Jerusalem, but he listened politely whenever I talked about it.

"At every Passover Seder, there's a portion of the service in which we say, 'Next year in Jerusalem.' For centuries, when the memory of Jerusalem was just a distant flicker we could only dream about, these words were said as a prayer."

Though Mike was not a Christian, he seemed somewhat interested in what I had to say about the holy city, so I continued.

"Jerusalem has seen days of incredible glory and prominence on the earth. Solomon, the richest and wisest man who ever lived, built a spectacular temple of worship to God there that has never been matched and never will be. The temple of Solomon is where the *shekina* glory of God himself dwelt."

I doubted Mike knew the significance of that. He probably had no clue what the word *shekina* even meant. And I felt inadequate to explain it.

"After Solomon's reign, the Babylonians attacked and burned the city to the ground, and the temple with it. The Jews were exiled to Babylon, where once again they quoted the prayer of hope at their Passover Seders: 'Next year in Jerusalem.'"

In my mind, I could hear my family repeating that cherished phrase. It made me miss the family gatherings of my childhood, especially our Passover Seders.

"After seventy years of exile, their prayer was answered and the city was restored. The temple was eventually rebuilt, but it never reached its former fame or glory."

Oh, how I would love to have seen the original temple with all its splendor.

"In AD 70, the second temple was destroyed by the Romans, and the Jews were exiled to the Diaspora for almost two thousand years."

"That's so sad." Though Mike was not a Jew, I appreciated his compassion for my people.

"Even after the State of Israel was reborn in May of 1948, Jerusalem remained in Jordanian hands. We continued to pray in our synagogues and at our Passover Seders the hope that Jerusalem would be restored to us again."

"And it was, right?"

I smiled. "In 1967, for the first time in more than two thousand years, our Passover prayer became a reality. During the Six-Day War, Israeli troops under the famous one-eyed general Moshe Dayan recaptured the city and brought it back into Jewish hands. Though the prayer continues to be a tradition every Passover Seder, any Jew can go to Jerusalem any time he or she wants to now."

"You obviously have a tremendous passion for that place. But why?"

"It's hard to explain. Maybe because it's the heart and soul of the Jewish nation. And the name of the God of Israel is irrevocably connected to that city."

"How often do you visit there?"

"Every chance I get. I've been there at least ten times so far, but I'd love to go back again."

If I closed my eyes, I could visualize the new Jerusalem, the modern part of the city that was outside the Old City. I especially loved Ben Yehuda Street, where no cars were allowed and everyone walked on foot. Lots of young people hung out there, religious and secular alike. Jews from all around the world, speaking many different languages, all called it home.

I missed the sights, the smells, the shouting, the nonstop activity, the falafel stands, the taxis, even the young soldiers milling around with rifles casually slung over their shoulders. The place was a constant hive of activity, often right up to midnight and even beyond.

But I loved visiting the Old City of Jerusalem even more. The moment I entered Jaffa Gate, I left the modern world and was instantly transported into an ancient time. Both temples had once stood within those walls, where the Temple Mount was now. Armenian Orthodox priests, who wore almost sinister-looking black priestly vestments, had churches in that area. Thousands of orthodox Jews lived there, many wearing the traditional Chassidic black clothing that was worn by rabbis in Eastern Europe centuries earlier. At the Western Wall, the last remaining outer wall of the second temple, people from all around the world wrote prayers on pieces of paper, folded them, and stuffed them into the cracks of the stones in the hope that the God who watches over that city would notice them, hear from heaven, and answer their prayers.

Just beyond the Western Wall was the Golden Dome of the Rock and Al Aksa Mosque, built in the sixth century AD near where the ancient temples once stood—perhaps on the very site itself. Many Muslims prayed in that place, believing that Abraham had offered up

Ishmael there, instead of Isaac. They also claimed that this was where Mohammed had been seen ascending to heaven.

No orthodox Jew dared go there, at least not while wearing their traditional outfits, because the hostility would be too great. Yet it was only a few hundred feet from the Western Wall, the last remaining retaining wall of the second temple, where thousands of orthodox Jews prayed day and night.

Mike cleared his throat, reminding me of his presence.

I opened my eyes with a sigh. "Jerusalem is a city of passions and contradictions. People from all over the world visit it on religious pilgrimages year in and year out, hoping this ancient city will bring them closer to God. And most find his imprint as indelibly marked in their hearts as it is on the very stones of the city."

Mike grinned. "You've described the place in so much detail, I almost feel like I've been there."

I sighed. "No one can really know the city without actually going there." A sudden thought made my heart leap. "I should take you! I'd love to show you around so you can experience Jerusalem yourself."

He didn't seem too thrilled with the idea. But for the next several days, I pestered him enough that he finally agreed.

MY JERUSALEM ENCOUNTER

Mike and I took a day off work at the kibbutz and caught a bus to Jerusalem.

"I can hardly wait to take you to the Arab market just inside the Jaffa Gate of the Old City. In the *shuk*, the bargaining process can become quite intense. You can get seriously overcharged if you don't play your cards right. So if you find something you like, let me know—outside the hearing of the vendors—and let me do all the talking."

I eagerly anticipated doing some serious bartering when we got there. That bus could not move fast enough for me.

"The last time I was at the market, I bought a solid brass tea set on an ornate brass tray. I gave it to my mom as a gift. She's displayed it in her living room for years." I hoped to find something just as nice this time. "The vendor started off asking a very high price, so I walked away. He called me back seven times, making a lower offer each time, until he finally said that if he went any lower he wouldn't make any money on the deal. That's when I knew I could buy it. I got the whole set for about thirty dollars."

Mike whistled, obviously impressed with my bargaining skills.

The bus dropped us off near Ben Yehuda, in the center of Jerusalem, and we walked the rest of the way to the Jaffa Gate entrance to the Old City.

As I approached the huge wooden gate, I recalled Frank telling me that Jesus had spent a lot of time in Jerusalem. In that moment, I had the strangest thought: this was the City of Jesus. Because I'd been raised on Jewish history, I knew Jerusalem as the City of David. But I felt strangely warmed by the idea that this was the City of Jesus.

After Mike and I walked through the Jaffa Gate, we took an immediate left and made a beeline for the shuk. When we were about halfway there, suddenly, standing right in front of me, I saw Jesus of Nazareth.

I stopped dead in my tracks. He was looking directly at me, with the most incredible brown eyes I had ever seen. I felt like rivers of liquid love were flowing from him into me.

I turned to Mike, who was standing to my left. I was about to grab his arm and say, "Look, there's Jesus!" But Mike didn't see him. Neither did anyone else around us. It was as if they were all frozen in time, and Jesus and I were there alone, just the two of us.

As I gazed at him, transfixed, I immediately knew three things. First, he looked distinctly Jewish, with olive skin and Middle Eastern complexion, dressed in robes and sandals like people wore two thousand years ago. That caught me off guard. It had never crossed my mind that Jesus was a Jew.

All the stained-glass windows I'd seen in churches depicted Jesus as an austere, European-looking man with a golden plate around his head. The paintings I'd seen from the Renaissance and the Middle Ages looked nothing like the Jesus standing before me now. In Leonardo Da Vinci's "The Last Supper," Jesus and his disciples all looked like Swedish choirboys—except Judas, the betrayer, who looked like an exaggerated Jewish caricature.

The second thing I immediately knew was that he was more than just a man. As a Jew, I knew I should not be having this thought, but I could not deny that this was the case.

The third thing I realized instantly was that he knew everything about me, including every sin I had ever committed or ever would commit, but that did not change his unconditional love for me one iota. He gazed at me like I was the only person in the universe. I had his full, undivided attention. I was enraptured by his love, beyond anything I had ever experienced.

Without opening his mouth, he spoke a word to me audibly in Hebrew: *Hineni,* which means "Here am I." I knew he was saying that he was the one I'd been searching for, even though I didn't know it. Every relationship I had tried, all the women, the fighting, the struggle for identity and significance, was all wrapped up in him. I sensed in my heart that he was the answer to my every need and any question I'd ever had. I felt complete and whole and fully accepted for the first time in my life.

Then, just as suddenly as he had appeared, he disappeared into thin air. I stood rooted to that spot, unable to move. But I frantically looked around for him.

Suddenly, about ten feet to my right on the cobbled brick road, he reappeared, looking at me with those incredible brown eyes that were like rivers of living water. Again I felt like I was the only person in the universe and I had his full, undivided attention. I never wanted this moment to end. After twenty-two years of striving for answers, my search was finally over.

I couldn't see Mike or anyone else. It was as if I were in a different dimension, where the unseen was visible and the visible became unseen. I never wanted to leave this place.

Without warning, he disappeared again. Frantic, I looked around for him again. Only when he was there did I feel complete. I couldn't live without him.

Directly in front of me was a wall about thirty feet high. The top of the wall was wide and flat enough to walk on, with parapets between huge stones. The sporadic openings had been designed for soldiers to shoot at invading enemies.

When I saw Jesus walking along the top of the wall, my heart leaped. This time he wasn't facing me, but looked directly in front of him as he walked. That disturbed me. I wanted him to gaze at me like I was the only person on the planet, like he'd done the previous times. I wanted to holler, "Jesus, here I am!" But the words would not come out. So I cried out from the depths of my being, like a silent prayer, "Oh, how I wish he would look at me just one more time."

The instant I had that thought, Jesus came to one of the openings between the huge stones. He turned his head and looked into my eyes with a piercing, penetrating, deliberate gaze, as if to say, *The moment you had that thought, it was like a prayer to me, and now I am answering you.*

As soon as I heard those words in my heart, he disappeared. This time I instinctively knew I would not see him again.

Suddenly, I was back in the hustle and bustle of Jerusalem with my friend.

"Come on, Geoff," Mike said. "Let's go. It's time to do some bargaining in the market."

I followed my buddy, pretending nothing had happened. I couldn't tell him what I'd just seen. He'd think I was nuts. Besides, I had no idea how to explain the vision I'd experienced.

I had no clue what to do next, so I focused the best I could on carrying on like normal. Yet I knew, deep down, that "normal" as I had known it would never be possible again.

I tried bartering, but felt as if I were just going through the motions. I had a new and wonderful secret, yet I was too scared to share it with anyone. I had seen Jesus, who was supposed to be dead. And I must be the only Jew who had ever seen him.

I couldn't tell anyone what had happened. They'd think I was weird or hallucinating. I'd never been into drugs. I wasn't even a heavy drinker. Oh, I'd smoked dope a few times with a few girlfriends, but I didn't particularly enjoy it. I hated the idea of losing full control over my mental faculties, so I never made it a habit.

But this experience with Jesus had been real. In fact, it was more real than anything I'd ever experienced in my life.

One burning question filled my heart: what was I to do with Jesus?

BACK TO THE USA

The rest of my time in Israel was a blur. As I rode the bus back to Shefayim, I decided to confide in Frank, hoping he would understand since he'd told me Jesus spent a lot of time in Jerusalem. But when I got back to the kibbutz, I discovered he had returned to the US.

I decided to go back to New York myself, right away. Americans didn't seem to have anti-Semitism ingrained into them like the Europeans or the South Africans. In my opinion, they were a kinder, more compassionate nation.

Besides, things were strained between me and Katrina. And with Frank gone I wasn't going to get any of my questions answered. I hoped someone in New York could help me.

— •◆• —

When I got back to New York, I decided to go to FIT to change my major to Fashion Buying and Merchandising for the following semester.

As I was walking down Fashion Avenue toward FIT, I saw a guy handing out pamphlets to people. The back of his T-shirt had "Yeshua" printed in bold letters. When he turned around, I saw the front of his shirt, which said, "He's Jewish."

Putting two and two together, I figured that Yeshua must be Jesus' Hebrew name. Since I had just come to that realization in Jerusalem, I was stunned at this bizarre coincidence.

Who was this person handing out tracts, and how could he know what I had just realized through my personal encounter with Jesus?

I recalled a time when I was fourteen, and my family was on vacation in Cape Town at a beautiful beach at Clifton. I saw people with "Jews for Jesus" T-shirts handing out pamphlets and talking to people. Curious, I wanted to speak to them, but my father warned me to stay away. "They are Christians who want to convert Jews," he said. "You must never get into a conversation or argument with them, because you could never win. They are highly trained deprogrammers. If you spend any length of time with them, you will get brainwashed and possibly even end up becoming a Christian!"

Because I admired him and knew he had a lot of wisdom, I'd taken what he said to heart. I figured he must know what he was talking about.

I decided to avoid the guy handing out the tracts. But I had to walk around him in order to get to the FIT registration office. As I passed by, he shoved a pamphlet into my hand.

I noticed other people throwing them on the ground. Some tore them in half first. They must have heard about these guys' brainwashing techniques. Not wanting to be a litterbug, I looked for a trash can. Not seeing one close by, I continued walking.

Out of curiosity, I glanced at the tract. It looked rather unprofessional, as if some wannabe artist had used a black marker to sketch an animated Jewish bearded face. I opened the pamphlet and found a message that looked like it had been handwritten in black marker. At the end of the text, the author was identified by the name Baruch Goldstein. I cringed. The word *baruch*, which means "blessed" in Hebrew, was used for Sabbath blessings over the bread, the wine, and the candles. Who on earth would name their child that?

What a twisted Christian plot this was, I thought, drawing a bearded Jewish caricature and giving him such an exaggerated Jewish name as Baruch Goldstein. My dad was right. These guys had to be avoided at all costs.

I closed the tract and threw it in the first trash bin I found.

After I'd changed my major at FIT, I headed for a travel agency on Park Avenue. Since I still had some time before classes started in the fall, I'd decided to visit an uncle and aunt of mine who had moved from Israel to Malibu. I had arranged to stay with them for the rest of the summer so I could watch the Olympics there. I hoped to see a lot of the boxing events, even though South African athletes had been banned from participating since we were being boycotted because of apartheid.

As I walked, I kept thinking about that tract and about "Jews for Jesus." Did these Christians have any idea what it would be like for a Jew to even consider becoming a believer in Jesus? Coming from a tight-knit community where everybody knew everyone else, I didn't know of a single South African Jew who would dare to do such a thing. After all, becoming a believer in Jesus would mean they were no longer Jewish, wouldn't it? Any Jew who said he believed Jesus was the Messiah would be ostracized from the community, kicked out of the synagogue, and most likely disinherited and declared to be dead by the family.

To Jews who were raised in an orthodox background, as most South African Jews were, accepting Jesus meant rejecting everything the Jews had ever lived and died for, everything we stood for as a nation. It was tantamount to turning your back on your people, and even your God. Jews who believed in Jesus were called *meshummad*, the Yiddish word for "traitor."

The more I thought about that pamphlet, the angrier I got. I decided to write to whoever wrote it and give him a piece of my mind. Remembering that the tract had an address on it, I turned around, walked back a few blocks to that trash can, pulled out the propaganda I'd thrown away, and shoved it into the front pocket of my jeans.

As I was about to enter the travel agency office, I saw another Jews for Jesus guy handing out pamphlets. These guys had a lot of nerve coming to the nicer parts of New York City and giving people tracts they were just going to tear up and litter the sidewalks with!

My fear of being brainwashed was overcome by my frustration about having no one to talk to about my dilemma. So I decided to walk up to that guy and ask him some questions. If he tried to give me one of his preprogrammed answers, I'd knock him out with a right cross to his jaw and leave him lying there. After all, if he was unconscious, he couldn't brainwash me. A brilliant plan! I'd do it so quickly and efficiently, no one would even notice until I was gone.

I marched toward my unsuspecting victim. When I got close, I noticed how Jewish he looked. These Jews for Jesus were so crafty, they even picked Gentiles who looked like Jews to do their dirty work. Clearly they would stop at nothing to convert a Jew.

I got right up close to his face and verbally unloaded on him. "Do you have any idea what it's like to be Jewish and to even *think* of believing in Jesus? The rejection, the persecution, the—"

"Yes, I do," he interrupted calmly. "I am Jewish and a believer in Jesus."

I was stunned. He didn't realize it, but he had given the only response that could have prevented me from knocking him out cold.

For some time, I'd been wondering if Jesus could possibly be the Messiah. And right there on Park Avenue in New York City, I'd bumped into the only other Jew I'd ever met who believed the same thing. I did have one cousin who claimed to believe in Jesus, but he'd been into so many Eastern religions before that, I didn't take him seriously.

For the first time in months I didn't feel alone. Here was someone I could speak to who would understand what I was going through. "You really are Jewish?" I asked.

He smiled. "Yes, I am."

"Does your family know that you believe in Jesus?"

His eyes took on a sad expression. "They disinherited me for my faith. Even had a mock funeral where they officially declared me to be dead."

That would undoubtedly be my family's reaction if I expressed faith in Jesus.

"But I believe there is a higher calling than seeking the approval and acceptance of men: the call to follow the truth that Jesus is the promised and long-awaited Messiah. No matter how inconvenient that truth happens to be."

In spite of the hefty price, I had to consider this important decision. If Jesus truly was the Messiah, sent by the God of Jacob to deliver Israel from their sins, I was obligated to follow him, regardless of what anyone thought about me. Surely loyalty to God and his word was more important than pandering to men's opinions, even if it meant rejection by my beloved brethren.

I had a serious choice to make. Would I live the rest of my life pleasing God or pleasing people?

I gazed at the man standing before me. Clearly he'd chosen a path that did not please his family. He had lost everything he'd valued the most because he was willing to follow and serve God.

"Are there other Jewish people who believe in Jesus?"

"Oh, yes. Lots of them. In fact, all the Jews for Jesus staff are Jewish."

All of a sudden I was open to hearing the gospel, but only through Jewish believers because of my distrust of Christians.

Could it be? I stared at the tracts in his hand. "What about … Baruch Goldstein?" I expected him to tell me the sketch on the pamphlet was merely a drawing, not a real person.

"Absolutely. You can meet him if you want to. He works in the New York branch of Jews for Jesus."

My heart skipped a beat. "How cool would that be, to speak to the guy who'd written these pamphlets.

Unfortunately, I had a trip scheduled. "I'm going to Los Angeles." I tilted my head toward the travel agency entrance. "For the Olympics."

"No problem." He grinned. "Jews for Jesus will be handing out tracts there too."

"Really? Maybe I'll look for them while I'm there."

"Great." He cupped my shoulder with his free hand. "I'd love to talk to you more, but I have a quota of tracts to hand out." He turned and resumed giving his pamphlets to passersby.

I had many more questions I wanted to ask. But both of us had things to do. So I walked into the travel agency, more eager than ever to make this trip to California.

LOS ANGELES

My aunt Rosalind, my mom's sister, welcomed me into her Malibu beach home with open arms and an open heart.

"Thanks for letting me stay with you." As a student with no income, I couldn't have afforded several nights at a hotel.

Her husband, my uncle, invited me to take a seat on the deck overlooking the ocean. We talked about the times I'd visited them when they lived in Israel. They had owned a factory there that made beautiful, handcrafted Jerusalem candles with stained-glass patterns in various colors.

I attended several Olympic games in LA during my visit. I kept an eye out for Jews for Jesus people handing out tracts, but didn't see any.

One evening, after returning to my uncle's home following a competition, I asked him what he thought about the possibility that Jesus might be the Messiah.

Though he wasn't a very religious person, he reacted with strong animosity. I decided to avoid any talk about Jesus while I was staying there. After all, I was no expert on the subject, not by a long shot.

While in California, I spent some time with a Jewish friend I'd met through Mike in New York. They'd played rugby together and he was a well-built, solid guy who was also extremely bright and gifted. After moving to LA, he built a budding law practice.

One day, as I was on a bus in Westwood, a pretty young woman caught my eye. I asked if she minded if I sat next to her, and she was happy to let me. The attraction between us was instant and mutual. We exchanged phone numbers.

Not wanting to bring a girl to my aunt and uncle's house, I called my lawyer friend. He told me he had a nice apartment in Beverly Hills that he wasn't using at the moment, and he was willing to let us go there.

I spent the night with this girl at this guy's place. It was a spur-of-the-moment thing, an attempt to fill a void in my life with any kind of love I could find, even if only for one night.

During my few weeks in LA, some friends offered me cocaine. I knew people in New York who were common users, but the drug scared me, so I avoided it. "I've heard it can take you on a real high, but you crash and have a bad low afterward. And when its effects wear off, you have to keep taking more to avoid the crash and the low. That's how people get addicted."

My friends scoffed. "That only happens when people use low-grade cocaine. But this is the purest stuff money can buy."

Against my better judgment, I decided to try it just once. I sniffed a few lines and immediately felt lightheaded, like I was floating through the roof. The thought of losing control frightened me.

I don't remember much after that until the high began to wear off. The crash they told me wouldn't happen hit me suddenly. I felt like the bottom of my stomach fell out. I couldn't stand, so I lay down on a bed. I regretted having tried this drug and swore I would never do anything so stupid again. I couldn't wait for the effects to be over so I could go back to feeling normal.

A deep depression hit me. Waves of hopelessness and despair washed over me, and I couldn't stop them.

An evil-sounding voice echoed from a deep pit inside me, as if it came from the very core of my being. *What if there is no God?*

I had never for a second contemplated such a possibility. In fact, I'd always felt sorry for people who were atheists or agnostics. I couldn't imagine life without the hope of God. It seemed such a pointless and empty existence. What was there to live for if there were no God?

I'd never experienced anything supernatural in my life, until a few weeks ago, when I saw Jesus and he spoke the word *Hineni* to me in a beautiful, gentle, holy voice. Now I was hearing a harsh, wicked voice that was trying to make me doubt the very existence of God.

I sensed there was a battle raging in my soul between two opposing forces vying for my loyalty. I felt like I was being dragged into a vortex I had opened myself up to by taking that drug.

I silently answered the dark voice in my mind. *If there is no God, there's no point in living. There's certainly no point in trying to do good. If there is no God, there's no moral foundation to strive for, no good or evil because it's all subjective. I might as well throw all restraint to the wind, because whether I live or die, it's all meaningless.*

The thoughts didn't even seem to be my own.

Then it hit me. Had I just heard the voice of the devil? And was he was trying to make me think there was no God? I didn't like the thought of that at all.

It seemed like this strong invisible force was trying to destroy me before I could find the answers I was looking for. I felt as if I were caught in the middle of a battle between good and evil, light and darkness.

When I was in the army, the enemy was clear and definable, and I could train and spar and work out to be able to beat him. But this enemy was invisible. I knew I could not defeat him on my own. Victory would require a supernatural solution. But I was more determined than ever not to let evil prevail.

14

FINALLY HOME

I really felt at home in the US. I never had to worry about anti-Semitism because racism of any kind was simply not tolerated. Sure, there were isolated pockets of it here and there, as there is in any country. But it was not the norm. And if it manifested as criminal behavior in any way, it would be prosecuted to the fullest extent of the law. I loved the respect for human life, and the dignity and freedom I found there.

Because of political instability in South Africa, and the anti-Semitism I experienced in the army, I hadn't felt like I had a home country since I was fourteen. Maybe, I thought, the US would be my home.

My father had always said, "As the US goes, so goes the world, because they are the leaders of the free world. So you might as well live in the US someday."

When my grandparents on my father's side left Lithuania in the early 1900s to escape the threat of death and persecution during the pogroms, they emigrated to the US. After their daughter Esther was born, they moved to South Africa to join the growing Lithuanian

Jewish community there. The first time I heard this, I wondered if I would find a home in the US myself one day.

The positive side to feeling as if I had no home country was that it motivated me to find security outside of my external circumstances. It drove me to find a "spiritual home" that no one could snatch away from me. I had come to realize that life was too short and too fragile not to find the purpose for which I was put on this planet. In the US, I sensed I was closer to finding "home" than ever before, and that somehow it was connected to Jesus.

One day, while I was staying with my aunt and uncle in Malibu for the summer, I managed to get a ticket to the Olympic boxing quarterfinals. I couldn't have been more excited. I took the bus to the stadium, and when I arrived, the atmosphere was electric.

As I was walking toward the boxing arena, I saw one of my childhood heroes: Floyd Patterson. He was the world heavyweight boxing champion before Mohammed Ali, and he had one of the best left hooks in boxing history. I had modeled my own left hook on his style. He was also one of the last true gentlemen of boxing, a tribute to the sport.

I walked up to him and said, "You're Floyd Patterson, right?"

"I sure am." He shook my hand warmly.

"I'm an avid student of the boxing world and a fighter myself," I told him. "And you were one of my childhood heroes."

He responded with a big, friendly smile.

I asked him about his fight with Mohammed Ali.

"You mean Cassius Clay," he said with derision in his voice. "I don't understand this name-changing business." Clearly he still didn't like the guy, even after so many years.

I thanked him for talking to me, then we went our separate ways. I walked on with a glow in my heart. I couldn't believe I'd met my old hero, and he was nice enough to give me his full attention, even though I was a total stranger.

As I neared the entrance to the stadium, I noticed a guy handing out tracts. He looked like a nervous Woody Allen type, with beady eyes and thick glasses, and he was wearing a "Jews for Jesus" T-shirt.

I eagerly approached him. "Hi. I'm Jewish, and I think Jesus might be the Messiah," I blurted out. "What can I do about that?"

He seemed shocked by my boldness and possibly thrown off by my accent. He'd probably never met a South African Jew. "I can't talk very long right now. I'm supposed to be handing out tracts to as many people as possible."

"Could I have your phone number so I can call you when you're free and ask you some questions about Jesus?"

He sized me up, taking in the black bandana tied around my forehead, my tank top with Hebrew lettering, and my muscular arms. After glancing around nervously, he whispered, "Look, I'm sorry if I seem paranoid. But we've been getting threats from the Jewish Defense League's anti-missionary wing. Some of us have even had our car tires slashed and rocks thrown through our windows."

I found it odd that this guy was scared of me, thinking I might be a plant for the JDL, trying to get his contact info so I could beat him up. Maybe I looked more intimidating than I thought.

"Why don't you give me your number and I'll call you?" he suggested.

I gave him the number at my aunt's house. "But when you call, don't say you're from Jews for Jesus." I was grateful that this organization existed, to help connect people like me to Jewish believers. But the name "Jews for Jesus" was scorned by the Jewish community. And a few weeks earlier, when I told my uncle I was considering the claims of Jesus, he'd gone nuts. He'd go ballistic if he knew I'd actually been talking to these people.

He agreed to my terms. "I'll just say I'm a friend."

THE CALL

After I got back to Malibu, I anxiously awaited this guy's call. When it finally came, he told me they were having a Bible study at their office in the San Fernando Valley on Tuesday night at seven. He invited me to come. When I said I was interested, he gave me the address.

I found out it was a long drive from Malibu to the Valley. I couldn't ask my aunt or uncle for a ride, so I'd have to get a car. But I didn't have a credit card, which was a requirement for a rental.

I flipped through the Yellow Pages and found a company called Rent a Wreck. It sounded scary. But it seemed like my only option, so I called.

They told me they had a vehicle available for eighty dollars for a week. They accepted cash and didn't require a credit card.

When I arrived at the rental place, they offered me a really old Ford Pinto. I had never seen one of those alive on the road. It was such a mess, I figured that explained why they didn't require a credit card. If I never brought the car back, I'd probably be doing them a favor.

But I was desperate to find answers. I had to go to that Bible study, no matter what I had to do to get there.

When I put my foot on the gas pedal, the car moved forward. The brakes seemed to work too. Reverse even functioned. So I paid the eighty dollars and putted down the road, with a plume of smoke trailing behind me. I hoped the cops wouldn't stop me. This wasn't South Africa, where I could talk my way out of anything. Plus, this heap of junk wasn't exactly a getaway car.

On Tuesday night, I gave myself an hour to get to the Bible study, but in LA traffic, that wasn't long enough. I finally arrived, a bit late, and parked outside the building.

When I walked in, people were singing with their hands lifted. They seemed really happy. The music sounded Jewish, and the songs all talked about Yeshua, which I had figured out was Jesus' name in Hebrew.

Most of the people were Mexicans, which surprised me. I concluded that Mexico must have really good relations with Israel. I was happy about that. We needed all the friends we could get.

I felt strangely at home there, and I hoped this would provide me with the last piece of the puzzle I'd been looking for. Here, Jews and Gentiles all worshipped the one true God of Israel together, which made perfect sense. It seemed so good and right to me that I joined in the singing. The whole experience felt so wonderful and natural, I couldn't imagine why anyone would not believe this.

After the singing ended, a small, balding Jewish guy with a high-pitched voice stood to share the message. Avi spoke about Jonah the prophet, and how God loved Gentiles and even reached out to them in Old Testament times.

I was surprised to hear that. Surely God loved Jewish people more. We were his chosen people. I'd always thought *chosen* meant "preferred."

I obviously had a lot to learn about what the Bible really said.

But I actually liked the idea that God loved all of humanity, and that he didn't choose just one group of people and ignore the rest.

After the service Avi came up to me and said hi. "What brought you here today?" he asked.

I told him about the guy I'd seen handing out tracts with the sketch of someone supposedly named Baruch Goldstein on the cover.

"Mr. Goldstein is a real person," he assured me. "He lives in New York. He's the branch manager of our ministry there. And he really is Jewish."

I determined to find that man and meet him when I got back to the East Coast.

"Do you believe that Jesus is the Messiah of Israel?" Avi asked.

I thought about Psalm 22, and my vision of Jesus in Jerusalem. "I do," I said, surprised at my own strength of conviction.

"Have you ever prayed to receive God into your heart?"

What kind of strange question is that? I wondered. How could God fit into my heart? He was high and holy and big, and my heart was tiny in comparison. I had no idea what he was talking about. Completely confused, I stared at him blankly. "No."

He invited me to his office. I followed him and sat by his desk.

Avi opened his Bible to a book called Romans, which I thought was an odd name for a book of the Bible. "I'd like to read to you what it says in chapter ten, verse nine." He looked reverently at the page before him. "If you confess with your mouth, 'Jesus is Lord,' and believe in your heart that God raised him from the dead, you will be saved."

Saying, "Jesus is Lord," seemed simple enough. But believing that God had raised him from the dead was a hard pill to swallow. I'd never heard of such a thing. Was that what Christians believed? If Jesus wasn't even dead anymore, why on earth were they so mad at the Jews? Had we really been persecuted for centuries for killing a man who wasn't even dead? This was really getting confusing.

I thought it through carefully. If Jesus had risen from the dead, surely he must be the Messiah. I didn't know if I had enough faith to believe this. But I did believe he was the Messiah. So I decided to accept the "resurrection" part by faith and agreed to pray the prayer.

I closed my eyes. "Jesus," I said, "I believe you are the Messiah. And I believe that God raised you from the dead. Amen."

When I opened my eyes, Avi jumped up and hugged me. "Brother, if you walk out of this building now and a truck hits you, you will go straight to heaven!"

What a strange little man this is, I thought. Why would he say something like that to me? I was always very careful when crossing roads, and I would never walk in front of a truck. Maybe he said it because he knew I was from a country where we drive on opposite sides of the road to the USA and therefore figured I was more prone to getting hit by a truck.

But the second part of his statement was even more confusing. If a truck hit me and I died as a result, that would be okay because I would go to heaven? I was going to heaven anyway. After all, I was one of God's chosen people. And not just any chosen person, but a direct descendant of the holy priesthood. I'd always thought my entrance to heaven was automatic and fully guaranteed.

A NEW LIFE

After the Bible study I drove my rental wreck back to Malibu. I knew something major had just happened in my life. I felt joyful and at peace. But I couldn't tell my uncle and aunt about this. I had no idea how to explain my new faith in Jesus.

I needed to get more established in my faith before I shared it with other people, especially in Jewish circles. I had no clue how to do that, but figured a good first step would be to get a Bible.

As I was wondering where I could find one, I saw a church just ahead of me on the road. It had a steeple and a cross on the roof. What better place to get a Bible than a church?

I pulled into the parking lot and opened the door. I found rows of empty pews with red books that said Hymnal on the covers, but no Bibles. I walked down the aisle. Finally I saw a Bible lying on one of the pews in the front row. I reached for it. But then I realized I couldn't just take it. That would be stealing.

I felt like I had just past some kind of test. I needed a Bible so I could understand what had just happened to me. But I knew the Ten Commandments, so I could not steal the Word of God.

I walked out of the church and back to my car. I'd just have to find a church that would give me a Bible.

When I got back to Malibu, I was so excited about my experience I had to tell someone about it. So I went to visit my Jewish lawyer friend in Beverly Hills. He was a bright and open-minded young guy.

As I told him what had happened, he listened intently.

"I feel different," I told him. "Like there's someone new living inside me, moving and guiding me. And it feels pure and holy and everything feels new and brighter." I later found out this was the Holy Spirit. At the time, I didn't even know there was such a thing.

"I have discovered who the promised Messiah of Israel is! Jesus of Nazareth fulfilled all the Law and the Prophets. Accepting him into my life is the most incredible thing that has ever happened to me."

"That's very interesting," he said. "And I'm happy you've found your path in life. But I don't have any interest in taking this any further for myself, at least not at this point."

My heart sank. I had expected him to be as excited as I was about the prospect of discovering the Messiah and eternal life.

A few days later, I was in Westwood and an attractive woman in her thirties asked me to go to bed with her. I immediately knew this was another test. So I quickly got myself out of the situation.

Later, a friend said he had some good-quality dope and asked if I wanted to smoke with him. I said no. "I'll never smoke another joint or take another drug in my life," I told him. "I don't need it anymore."

The void I'd had in my life for years had been filled, and I didn't have to use anything artificial to satisfy me. Who needs dope when you can have the kind of joy and peace I knew? I couldn't imagine why anyone would not want to experience what I had.

No one gave me a lecture on all the sins and vices I would have to give up or a list of rules I had to keep because I was now a believer. I didn't need that. Because I had the Holy Spirit living in me, I knew intuitively what was right and wrong in any given situation, and he gave me the grace to choose what was right. Even though I sometimes stumbled, as a baby in the faith usually does, he was always gentle and forgiving. I feel really sorry for believers who think walking with Jesus is following a list of rules and regulations.

When I read Jeremiah 31:34, where God says, "They shall all know Me, from the least of them to the greatest of them," I knew that by following Jesus I was now living out that ancient prophecy. I knew God personally, and he was leading and guiding my every step.

I determined to spend the rest of my life telling people about this incredible new life I'd just received.

When I got back to New York at the end of the summer, I connected with Baruch Goldstein. We got along great. He was a jolly, bearded, thickset guy. And he was a Vietnam veteran and pretty tough. I felt I could relate to him. I also respected him.

He took me under his wing. Over the next several months, he helped me understand my faith better. He gave me some key Scriptures to memorize, and he taught me that Bible memorization was an important foundation of my faith. "The most powerful weapon you could ever have is to hide the Word of God in your heart."

When I told him I didn't own a Bible, he told me he'd take me to get one. To my surprise, he didn't go to a church but to the International Bible Society, where he bought me an easy-to-read English version.

"Scripture memorization will help you through the toughest trails," he assured me, "and keep you strong through the persecutions and opposition you'll have to endure from your Jewish brethren."

I knew the next major hurdle that loomed ahead for me would be sharing my faith with my parents. I felt indebted to him for helping me get established in my beliefs.

When I shared my newfound faith with one of the South African Jewish students I roomed with, he was furious. "You don't need that Jesus religion."

"That's just it," I said. "It's not religion. Having a personal relationship with God is an exciting adventure."

He shook his head. "Geoff, you're popular, and chicks dig you.

Why would you of all people need this born-again stuff? That's for the down-and-out, drug addicts, or people in prison who need God as a crutch."

"That's not true," I said. "Jesus is for everybody."

He gripped my shoulder. "Geoff, you'll go to hell for believing this."

I smiled. "It's strange you would say that, because the exact opposite happened. I've been saved from hell, where I would have gone without Jesus."

He sighed and left the room.

I knew our relationship would never be the same. My faith had created a wedge between me and the rest of the South African Jewish community at my college in New York. I wondered if that would always be the case.

I understood now why Avi had been so excited when I received Jesus. It wasn't that he thought I was careless at crossing roads. He realized that I had crossed from death to life by receiving Jesus as my Messiah.

———•—•———

I needed to put some things right in my life now that I was a believer.

When I told my girlfriend, Sarah, about my newfound faith, she listened respectfully but didn't seem very excited about it. She expected to spend the night with me, as she had often done in the past, but I told her we couldn't have sex anymore since, according to the Bible, it was wrong outside of a marriage relationship.

She was not happy about that. "You're taking this too seriously, Geoff."

But I would not be moved. I knew clearly now what was right and wrong, because I had the Bible to give me guidelines, and I had the Holy Spirit to lead and guide me. I had also received a lot of great insights from Baruch.

"I can't spend the night with you even without having sex."

Her eyes went wide. "Why not?"

"Because my roommates would presume we were having sex. And I must avoid even the appearance of evil."

Since my relationship with Sarah was pretty much only about sex, when that ended, so did the relationship. But our breakup didn't bother me. I had a whole new life and a great adventure before me.

I told my roommate he shouldn't be having sex with his fiancée until after they were married.

"Who are you to tell me that?" he bellowed. "You've been promiscuous as long as I've known you, and all of a sudden, just because you're abstaining, you expect me to do the same?"

"Look, I know this might come across as self-righteous. But I know better now."

He rolled his eyes and stormed out of the room.

I hadn't handled the situation well at all. But this was all so new to me. I needed a lot of wisdom to know what to say to people in the future. I was a baby believer, stumbling along as best I knew how.

I needed to be with other believers as much as possible, especially those who had been in this walk for a long time and were mature and established in their faith. I had a lot to learn, but I wanted to soak it all in like a sponge.

POWER FROM ABOVE

About a week after I got back to New York, I was invited to go on a full-day boat trip up the Hudson River with other Messianic believers, both Jews and Gentiles. It sounded like fun, especially since I'd been getting a lot of persecution from the South African Jewish community in New York that I'd been part of for the last year. They didn't like the new Geoffrey who had suddenly become a "Jesus freak." They preferred the womanizing Casanova version of me much more.

I took a taxi to the boat launch. I really wanted to share my newfound faith with the driver, but I couldn't get the words out. This bothered me a lot because I was not the timid type.

On the boat, I met a woman called Martha who was a strong believer. Faith and joy just exuded from her. I felt like I could trust her.

As we sat on the top deck, enjoying the sunny, early September day, I told her about my experience with the taxi driver. "I don't understand it. I wanted to share my faith, but it felt like I was missing something."

She opened her Bible and showed me numerous New Testament Scriptures that talked about baptism in the Holy Spirit. I had no clue what that was.

"After Jesus ascended to heaven, the early Jewish disciples were told to tarry in the city of Jerusalem until they were imbued with power from on high before they went out to preach the gospel."

She asked if she could lay hands on me and pray for me to receive this baptism in the Holy Spirit.

I had no idea what that was, but if it was in the Bible, I wanted it. So I immediately said yes. I knew there would be more persecution and tough times ahead for me. I hadn't even told my parents yet. I needed all the power available to me.

She stood behind my chair and laid her hands on my shoulders. I closed my eyes and bowed my head.

As she prayed, even though my physical eyes were closed, my spiritual eyes were opened. I saw the heavens open and a bright light in the form of a dove descend on me like a lightning bolt. I felt as if a thousand volts of electricity hit me, yet it didn't hurt me. On the contrary, it charged my whole being with life and power.

In that moment, I knew I was a changed man. I would never be afraid to share my faith again. I was filled with boldness and confidence to proclaim my faith wherever I went.

This was an all-or-nothing deal for me. I would never go back to my old ways, but instead would go all the way in my newfound faith. I didn't want to do anything except preach the gospel for the rest of my life. Everything else seemed meaningless.

CALLED TO PREACH

From that day on, I was unstoppable. I still lacked wisdom in many cases, but I shared the gospel wherever I went with whoever I could find. People either avoided me or they ended up giving their hearts to Jesus.

A lot of Jewish believers tend to be rather timid about sharing their faith with their brethren. But I wasn't. I had just discovered the Messiah of Israel, for whom I'd waited my whole life. I couldn't help but share this good news with whoever would listen. I had to tell every Jew I could that the Messiah they'd been waiting for two thousand years had already come and that he would one day come again.

When the Jews for Jesus people heard about me, they asked me to hand out tracts on the street and wear one of their T-shirts. I did it a few times, though I felt silly wearing the shirt.

One day, as I was handing out tracts with a few others, the Holy Spirit spoke to me clearly. "I have not called you to hand out tracts. I have called you to preach the gospel."

I immediately went to the leader of our group and told him what the Lord had just told me.

"We don't preach on the streets," he said simply. "We just hand out tracts."

"I'm not against anyone handing out tracts," I said. "But I have to do what God has called me to do."

I gave him my handful of pamphlets, took off the T-shirt, and returned it to him. He wished me God's best, and off I went.

But I had no idea where I could preach or how.

I went to Times Square, where an African-American woman named Brenda had a table and a sound system. While she preached about Jesus, three of four others handed out gospel tracts and talked to folks who had questions. Crowds of people passed by every day, especially during lunchtime and rush hour. Most of them didn't seem exactly thrilled by this. Times Square was a rough place, full of seedy peep shows. Drug dealers, pimps, and prostitutes hung around the area. What a tremendous need there was here for the gospel.

I had spoken to Brenda a few times, and we got along really well. As I stood there watching her preach, I wondered if I should join her. What would my college professors or my peers think if they saw me preaching on the street? I had a reputation for being a cool and cultured guy. It would be embarrassing for them and for me.

Even as these thoughts raced through my mind, I knew God was calling me to this. I had to put my reputation aside and just obey.

I remembered reading in the Bible that Jesus made himself of no reputation. I had to care more about obeying God's voice than having the approval and acceptance of men.

So I plucked up the courage and went to speak to Brenda.

When I asked if I could join her, she smiled, handed me the microphone, and said I could give it a try.

It was about five p.m. and rush hour, with thousands of people passing by every hour. They could hardly wait for the stoplight to change so they wouldn't have to listen to us anymore.

When I opened my mouth to speak, my knees felt weak. But the more I preached, the more natural it seemed. Words just poured out of my mouth. Scriptures I had memorized came to mind as I spoke, and I quoted them with power and authority.

Some people actually stopped to listen to this white guy with a Jewish-African accent. Others crossed the road as quickly as they could. A few even put their hands over their ears. Was I that bad?

When I finished for the day, Brenda told me she was impressed. "You can preach here anytime you want."

I was hooked. I went back to Times Square after classes every day and preached. People shouted at me, argued with me, but hardly a day passed that I didn't lead someone to the Lord right there on the street. I loved people and they could tell.

I still hadn't told my parents. I didn't want to break the news to them over the phone. It would totally freak them out. Though I had no idea when I'd be going to South Africa next, I felt it was important to tell them face-to-face.

One day, while I was preaching in Times Square, a pimp came by with a young girl he was using as a prostitute. She was clearly hooked on drugs, and she looked really out of it. All of a sudden, the Spirit of God rose up in me with righteous indignation. I looked at the guy and said, "If you want to go to hell, that's your choice, but don't take innocent young girls there with you. What you're doing is evil!"

I hadn't planned on confronting him in such a bold and direct way. But I felt that if Jesus were standing there, that was exactly what he would have said.

The pimp glared at me and reached under his jacket. I saw a pistol in a holster hung from his belt. "I'm going to shoot you right now!"

The crowd gasped.

"Go ahead," I said over the loud speaker. "Shoot me in front of all these witnesses. If you kill me, I know where I'm going. But if you keep abusing and using young girls, you'll end up in hell!"

He looked at me, then at the crowd, and marched off, apparently deciding it was in his best interests not to pull out his gun after all.

I realized my words seemed harsh, but I knew Jesus was speaking to him through me. God is love, but he hates seeing the strong take advantage of the weak and vulnerable.

From that time on, I was totally hooked on street preaching. I went to the roughest areas and preached with a microphone. The drug dealers told me to shut up, but I didn't care what they said. Since they didn't want the cops to see them, they moved to another area. But as I continued to preach on the streets, I saw many drug dealers give their hearts to the Lord.

Street preaching was scorned and despised by many, even by a lot of Christians. But I had so much love and passion for people, I didn't care what anyone thought of me. These people I was reaching would never go into a church or listen to the gospel on television, so I had to bring the message to them. And people were turning from darkness to light, from hell to heaven. I couldn't think of anything more rewarding to do with my life.

I knew, even in those early years of my faith, that one day I would preach this message all around the world and eventually reach millions with the good news of forgiveness of sin and eternal life. And I was not ashamed!

15

THE LETTER

My last obstacle to overcome was breaking the news of my faith in Jesus to my parents.

In Jewish circles it is considered perfectly acceptable and even normal to follow an Indian guru or Eastern religions and philosophies, which are very different from Judaism. But if someone brings Jesus into the picture, tension and controversy instantly erupt. The name of Jesus evokes strong reactions, especially when it comes to receiving him into your heart, following him, and becoming his disciple.

But that response only served to reinforce and galvanize my newfound faith. If Jesus was not the Messiah, no one would care whether I followed him or not. The fact that Jesus caused such an intense reaction of shock and opposition confirmed to me that I was on the right path.

The truth has never been popular. Moses was persecuted by the Israelites. On a number of occasions they even wanted to stone him. Elijah, Jeremiah, Isaiah, and all the major prophets were opposed by the majority in Israel. Why should I expect that anything had changed in modern times? Human nature is still the same.

There is a strong emphasis in Jewish circles about the importance of being open-minded … except when it comes to Jesus. It's considered narrow-minded or dogmatic to say he is the only way. But if he really is the only one who can forgive our sins, shouldn't we be grateful that God loves us so much, despite our fallen condition, that he sent a solution?

I wasn't too concerned about my mother's reaction to the announcement of my newfound faith. We had discussed spiritual matters in the past and she was more open-minded than most in the Jewish community.

But I was deeply concerned about my father's reaction. I loved and honored him, and I wanted him to always be proud of me.

I decided to write a letter telling them about my decision to follow Jesus and explaining why I'd done so. I described in detail how Jesus had fulfilled the messianic prophecies, which proved he was the promised Messiah. I even wrote about his future return to Israel, when he would rule and reign from Jerusalem for a thousand years.

I wondered if that last part might be too much. My dad would probably think I'd lost my mind when he read that. But I left it in anyway.

After mailing the letter, I waited with trepidation for the response. I checked the mailbox every day. And whenever the phone rang, I expected it to be my parents.

One day, I did get a call from my dad. He told me he was coming to New York for a business trip and wanted to get together with me. I wondered if he really had work here or if that was just an excuse to confront me face-to-face.

When he arrived, I brought him to my apartment and introduced him to my roommates. Then we took a walk around the neighborhood.

We hadn't gone more than a few blocks before he launched into the subject that was heavy on both our hearts. "I spoke to our rabbi about your letter."

I held my breath.

"He believes you've been brainwashed by that cult, Jews for Jesus. He told me I need to do whatever I can to persuade you to come back into the Jewish faith."

"Actually, Dad, I believe I have done that very thing by accepting Yeshua as Messiah. I feel closer to my Jewish roots than I ever have in my life. I'm now following the Jewish Messiah with all my heart. I've come back to the God of Israel by following his anointed one."

My father walked on without saying a word, but I could feel the tension build between us.

He finally broke the awkward silence. "The rabbis say you were lonely and vulnerable when you came to New York City. The Jews for Jesus people showed you love and acceptance. They weakened your resistance until you succumbed to their indoctrination. Then they 'converted' you and you became a … a Christian."

I understood his perspective. To the Jewish mind, *Christian* is the antithesis of everything Jewish. Jews have been persecuted and even murdered in the name of Christianity for centuries, from the Crusades of the eleventh century to the Spanish Inquisition to the pogroms of Eastern Europe. Most of these atrocities were committed under the guise of Christianity.

Of course, such horrors are far from who Jesus is. His whole life personified love, from his birth to his death on the cross. So while I was not ashamed of my fellow believers who called themselves Christians, I could not call myself by that name, at least not among my fellow Jews.

"I haven't 'converted,' Dad. That would imply leaving my Jewish faith. But that's not what happened. I've actually come back to the God of Israel though the Messiah. I haven't left my Jewish roots. I've returned to them. I am now a completed or fulfilled Jew."

"That's just further evidence that you've been brainwashed." He looked at me with love and sorrow. "Son, you're lost."

"No," I replied with fervent passion. "You're the one who's lost."

"No, you are!"

"No, you are!"

Obviously, this was going nowhere, so I stopped arguing.

We found a park and sat on a bench in silence for a few moments.

Finally my father handed me a slip of paper. "The rabbi gave me the phone number of some professional deprogrammers who live in Brooklyn. He wants you to spend a few days with them. They will show you where you have gone wrong."

Shortly before my dad arrived in New York, someone had given me a book called *Kidnapped for My Faith,* written by a Jewish believer who had literally been kidnapped by this group in Brooklyn. After a few days of deprivation and intense brainwashing, the author ended up denying his faith in Jesus. But he eventually came back to the Lord.

I knew I was too young in my faith to withstand the intense indoctrination and pressure these deprogrammers would expose me to. I might have to face them at some time in the future, but not now. I sensed the Holy Spirit warning me that I wasn't ready, and I trusted him implicitly.

My dad stared across the grassy field before us. "The rabbis believe that the reason you 'accepted Jesus' is because you don't adequately understand your Jewish roots."

I rolled my eyes. Had our rabbis brainwashed *him*? "Dad, I went to Jewish schools for most of my life. I laid tefillin five mornings a week and said all the Hebrew prayers. I was taught Jewish history and have lived in the Jewish faith all my life. You know what the rabbis told you isn't true."

"Then why have you been so easily influenced by these 'Jews for Jesus' people?"

I sighed. "I believed in Jesus before I met any of them. They just told me how to pray the prayer of salvation."

He looked me in the eye. "At the very least, you must be going through some kind of identity crisis if you don't even know who you are as a Jew anymore."

"This is not an identity crisis," I told him respectfully but firmly. "In fact, the opposite is true. For the first time in my life, I know who I am."

The hurt and fear in his eyes ripped at my heart.

"Look, if you want me to go to those deprogrammers, I'm willing to do it. But it will be for you, not for me."

The hope that sparked in his eyes filled me with fear as I recalled the details in that book I'd read. So before he could say anything more, I added, "I still have a temper, Dad. And if those guys try to so much as lay a hand on me, I promise you I'll knock them out."

I hated going back to my classic tactic of threatening to beat people up if I didn't like what they were doing. But I dreaded the thought of being taken by those deprogrammers.

"I can't tell you what to do," I told him. "I honor and respect you too much for that. So I've leave the decision in your hands."

We returned to my apartment in silence. While we made small talk for the rest of his visit, the subject of the deprogrammers was not brought up again.

After he left, I watched my back for months. Every time I saw a car or van with orthodox Jews in it, I tensed up, ready to resist any kidnapping attempt. It never happened. No one even called me.

I wasn't sure whether my father had decided not to contact them after all, or if God was miraculously protecting me. But I recalled a Bible verse I'd memorized that says, "God ... will not allow you to be tempted beyond what you are able, but with the temptation will also make the way of escape, that you can be able to bear it" (1 Corinthians 10:13). I stood on that Scripture, trusting that God would never allow me to go through anything that was beyond my ability to endure.

Because he made me, he knew exactly how much I could take and would never let me go beyond the grace he had given me. I was comforted to know that he was utterly faithful and reliable, so I had nothing to fear. As the Bible says, "If God is for us, who can be against us?" (Romans 8:31).

Although my family and I had a few more tense moments over the next few years because of my faith, my parents never disowned me because of my decision to follow Jesus. I had counted the cost when I decided to follow him, knowing my family might reject me. And God had honored that decision by giving my family back to me. We did have a few clashes over the path I chose, especially regarding my belief that Jesus is the only way to salvation. But we all took a mature approach and decided that nothing was worth breaking relationship over, and for that I was very grateful.

Scripture says, "Believe on the Lord Jesus Christ, and you will be saved, you and your household" (Acts 16:31). I am convinced that when God saves us, he not only wants us to reach the world with the gospel, but our families as well. In some cases, this requires breaking generations of unbelief.

The Bible indicates that one of the signs that Jesus' return is imminent is that the Jewish people will come back to their Messiah. Romans 11:15 says, "If their being cast away [the Jewish rejection of the Messiah] is the reconciling of the world [the Gentiles being reconciled to God], what will their acceptance be but life from the dead?" Jewish people are coming to know Jesus as their Messiah in greater numbers than we have seen since the first century. Hand-in-hand with this Jewish return to their God by embracing the Messiah, we are experiencing the greatest worldwide spiritual awakening ever seen to date, and it has only just begun.

MAISIE

I went back to South Africa in December, just a few months after my decision to give my heart to Jesus. While visiting with my family, nothing was said about my newfound faith. But at one point, my father mentioned that I had a second cousin named Maisie who was also a believer.

I was shocked. I had no clue that someone in my family had been a believer for decades.

I briefly wondered why my parents had never told me about Maisie. But then I realized they probably didn't want her to influence me toward what they viewed as "converting" to Christianity. Now that I was a believer too, my father kindly offered to put me in touch with her. I guessed he figured it was too late to do anything about it now, so he might as well introduce me to another believer in the family.

Although Maisie was technically a cousin, I'd always referred to her as my *aunty*, a term of respect and honor in the South African culture. She was about five-foot-two, with white hair and sparkling blue eyes that seemed to see right through me. She had a laugh that was infectious and a smile that radiated hope.

I could hardly wait to see her and talk about our shared faith.

When I visited her in her home, I discovered that she had become a believer in the 1930s, when it was unheard of for a Jew to believe in Jesus.

"When I was seventeen," she told me, "I had a coworker who was a born-again Baptist. I noticed that this young woman did not engage in idle chatter or laugh at the crude jokes in the office, but quietly did her work. After a few months I told this woman, 'There's something different about you. Can you tell me what it is?' She met with me after work. Because of the witness of her life, I became a believer too."

"How did your family react?" I asked.

"I was too terrified to tell them at first. So I kept my faith a secret for six months."

That didn't surprise me a bit. All of our relatives from Europe were very orthodox, and in those days, believing in Jesus would have been seen as a terrible betrayal.

"When I finally told my parents, my sister tried to strangle me to death. Just before I passed out, I managed to push her off."

I couldn't imagine either of my sisters trying to strangle me for my faith. But they couldn't have overpowered me anyway.

"Two years later I got a disease called *myishtenia gravis*, where all the muscles stop functioning. At that time it was incurable, and anyone who had it eventually died."

This was the first time I'd heard this about my cousin.

"I was in the hospital, sipping liquid food through a straw, when a pastor came into my room and told me he was going to pray all night with his church until he heard from God that I was going to be healed. I asked him why he would do that, and he responded that there was a great call on my life."

I hung on Maisie's every word, spellbound, as she shared this riveting story. I knew I had come back to South Africa to be discipled by a battle-proven warrior of the faith.

"The next day, the pastor came back. He said his church had prayed till about two in the morning. And then he heard the Lord say he had heard their prayers and was going to heal me so they could all go home now. I gradually improved and was eventually one hundred percent healed of this 'incurable' disease."

This had all happened in Maisie's late teenage years. Doctors told her she only had a few months to live, yet she was now in her eighties. She'd been in great health and serving the Lord for more than sixty years after her "death sentence" prognosis!

Clearly the supernatural power of God was the hallmark of Maisie's faith. I was greatly encouraged by this story, and I wanted to emulate her walk with God.

"I prayed for my sister and mother every day for eighteen years, and they eventually came to faith. In fact, my sister moved to Israel and spent years sharing her faith with the orthodox Jews in Jerusalem, proving to them from the Hebrew prophecies that Yeshua is the Messiah. My sister, who tried to strangle me for my faith and declared I might as well be dead for believing in Jesus, became a powerhouse for God as she testified among our people."

I admired Maisie's perseverance in prayer. At that moment I decided to pray for my family members with the same tenacity until every one of them came to know their Messiah.

"I became a spokesperson for the early messianic movement. I represented South African Jewish believers at International Alliance conferences for almost five decades. I was one of their top leaders worldwide. I was voted in as president of the Hebrew Christian Alliance in South Africa year after year."

Maisie had been a pioneer in the fledgling messianic movement, a spokesman for her people and her God. I longed to continue her legacy to the next generation.

"One of my greatest honors was becoming close friends with Corrie ten Boom, the Dutch Christian who saved hundreds of Jews from the Nazis until her family was betrayed and taken to concentration camps for their 'crime.' Whenever Corrie came to South Africa to speak and to tell people about her book, *The Hiding Place,* she always stayed at my home."

My Aunty Maisie was the best-kept secret in our family!

"When you were five years old, I went to Durban to visit your parents. I saw you playing in the backyard, and I prayed, 'Lord, I claim that little boy for your kingdom.'"

I felt as though Maisie were my spiritual mother. I believed God had protected me through the toughest times of my life through that prayer and her continued prayers for my salvation and that of my family.

GO TO AMERICA

About five years after I became a believer, I was in my grandmother Fruma's home in Johannesburg. At about five o'clock in the morning, I sat on the floor in the dark, with my back against the bed, praying. And God clearly told me, "Go to America. I am going to give you a wife there."

When I told my grandmother what I'd heard, she looked at me like I was nuts. I couldn't blame her. Sadly, in modern times Jewish people are not used to the concept of hearing God's voice directly, so to them it seems strange. But by that time in my walk I had learned that it was normal for God to speak to his children.

And if God said it, I was going to obey. It was that simple.

My father had recently been offered a position as president of an art-supply and picture-framing chain in Los Angeles, so my parents had already moved there. I decided to join them and work for my dad, using a management-training visa.

While there, I attended a wonderful church in LA led by Dr. Jack Hayford. Of the thirteen thousand members, about 10 percent were Jewish believers. Pastor Jack was a prolific teacher and a great lover of Israel. He was a pastor to thousands of pastors around the world, a leader of leaders. It was there, at a Monday night Bible study for singles where I met my wife.

Eight months after the day we met, we got married. I wanted her to meet Maisie and to get to know me better in my home country. So we moved back to South Africa. She had to adjust to our new life and many of my "South Africanisms." And I had to learn how to truly love a woman since I had only used them for my own pleasure in the past.

We lived in South Africa for the first two years of our marriage and had the privilege of serving the Lord side-by-side with Maisie. While we were there, I was voted chairman of the Hebrew Christian Alliance, and she was the treasurer.

BACK TO THE US

My wife and I had our first son in South Africa. After moving to the United States, we had two more boys. Ezra, Samson, and Joseph have become my best buddies. Each of them is incredibly gifted in his own field, and all of them are world changers in their own right. When God said to Abraham, "Surely blessing I will bless you, and multiplying I will multiply you," (Hebrews 6:14), he meant it! I have seen this in my own life and continue to see it in my family.

In 2006 I joined the staff of Gateway Church in Southlake, Texas, one of the fastest-growing churches in the US, with more than twenty-five thousand members. I served there for about nine years as the Messianic Pastor of Jewish Ministries.
Gateway strongly supports the principle of bringing the gospel to the Jewish people. The first Friday of every month, we had a messianic service, which became one of the largest gatherings of its kind in the nation. We regularly saw both Jews and Gentiles come to faith through this ministry.
I have been serving the Lord joyfully for more than thirty-three years now. I preach the gospel around the world, building bridges between my Jewish brethren and their Messiah and between them and the church. I speak at numerous conferences, sharing my testimony and teaching what the Bible says about Israel and God's plan for and covenant with the Jewish people. I am an evangelist with a pastor's heart and calling, and I have had the privilege of

leading thousands to the Messiah in both large and small gatherings.

I have even had the honor of preaching in the predominantly Muslim country of Indonesia, where I saw hundreds come to faith. I have begun to fulfill the call on my life and that of my people to truly be a "light to the Gentiles".

A few years ago I ministered at a national New Year's Eve celebration in Kampala, Uganda, to more than one hundred thousand people in person, plus a few million more via television. I have ministered in Argentina for more than twelve years now, and we are seeing a great move of God among Jews and Gentiles there as well as in South Africa, South Korea, Zambia, London, Switzerland, Germany, Belgium, Eastern Europe and more. People from all backgrounds, cultures, and religions are being swept into the kingdom. And the harvest has just begun!

I am just a simple guy from a small town in South Africa who heard the call of God and said, "Here I am. Do with me as you will." And just look at what he has accomplished in and through me by his grace alone.

He can do amazing things for you too. I am convinced that God is far more concerned with our availability than our ability. All you have to do is say, "Lord, use me for your glory," and you will see great and mighty things you never dreamed possible.

CONCLUSION

My coming to faith was only the beginning of what has been an ever- increasing and ever-expanding adventure. Even through many trials and tribulations, God has always shown himself to be faithful. My life as a believer has been filled with supernatural experiences and miracles that some might find hard to believe.

To tell you about all the amazing miracles God has done and continues to do in my life would easily fill a few volumes.

Walking in the supernatural became a way of life for me from the day I received Jesus. Because my first encounter with him was supernatural, I just came to expect it. I believe that how much you expect from God is how much you get—not in a greedy or self-fullling way, but by trusting him for great and mighty things to advance the kingdom, to plunder hell and populate heaven.

Paul the apostle said, " The gospel I preached is not something that man made up. I did not receive it from any man, nor was I taught it; rather, I received it by revelation from Jesus Christ" (Galatians 1:11–12). I too initially received the gospel as a revelation from Jesus. Even though the gospel is preached by men, it is God's message to mankind from beginning to end. He initiated it and he completed it.

Even though God mysteriously chooses to work through fallible people like myself, in the end the gospel message is about a perfect and holy God reaching out to imperfect humanity and giving his life for them. He can take the broken pieces of your life, as he did with me, and make it into something beautiful.

You are God's masterpiece and part of his plan, from your birth till your last breath. Your existence is not a mistake, regardless of the circumstances through which you were born. God began his work by bringing you into the world, and he will complete his plan for your life. All you have to do is yield to him.

I waited almost twenty-eight years to write this book. That's a long time to wait for anything. But I believe the reason for the delay was so that you could read this story at this particular time in your life so you can come to know the Messiah of Israel, the Savior of the world, in an intimate way.

I've shared my story and made myself vulnerable because of the love God has given me for people. Let me now share some closing thoughts with you.

FOR BELIEVERS

First, I would like to share a word with those who are believers in Jesus but who have had very little contact with Jewish people or the Jewish roots of your faith. Sadly, anti-Semitism is still rampant in many Christian circles. Sometimes it is subtle; other times it is outright and in the open. This attitude primarily comes from general ignorance and a misunderstanding of the Scriptures regarding God's eternal covenant with and purposes for the Jews. Often anti-Semitism is passed down from one generation to the next.

I am grateful for the emergence of a strong contingent of evangelical Christians who support Israel and the Jewish people. This movement is strongest in the US, but it is slowly spreading to other continents as well. In these times of rising anti-Semitism around the world, the Jews need their Christian brothers and sisters more than ever.

Jesus said in Matthew 25:40, "Inasmuch as you did it to one the least of these my brethren, you did it unto Me." How we treat people is how we are treating him, because we are all made in the image of God. But Jesus specifically mentioned "my brethren" here. Since he was a Jew, his brethren would be the Jewish people. How believers treat the Jews is equivalent to how they are treating Jesus.

Countless Jews have refused to consider Jesus as an option because of atrocities committed in his name by those who called themselves Christians. While I am now aware that those who perpetuated these horrors were not really Christians, most Jewish people don't know that. Because those who murdered or persecuted their families were members of churches and wore crosses around their necks, that makes them Christians in their eyes.

I urge you to examine what Jesus taught and the life he lived, and model that to your Jewish brethren. As Jesus said in Matthew 5:16, "Let your light so shine before men, that they may see your good works and glorify your Father in heaven."

You represent Jesus to the Jewish people in your circle of influence. You are the only "Jesus" many of them will ever see. Reflect God's passionate heart for his chosen people in your words and deeds. Scripture says the Jews are the "apple of His eye" (Zachariah 2:8). Jesus loved them so much that he willingly went to a cross in Jerusalem, where he died for their sins as well as those of all mankind. That is how much he loves the Jewish people.

The best way we can reflect the love of God to his people is by telling them that their Messiah, whom the Law and the Prophets foretold, has already come. Isaiah 53 contains a graphic foretelling of a suffering Messiah. Verses 3–4 say, "We hid, as it were, our faces from Him; He was despised, and we did not esteem Him. Surely He has borne our griefs and carried our sorrows." Psalm 22 said the Messiah would be crucified. Psalm 16:10 says, "You will not leave my soul among the dead or allow your holy one to rot in the grave" (NLT). Jesus fulfilled this prophecy when he rose from the dead three days after he was buried, thus conquering death and the grave and proving that he was God's Son. After the resurrection he appeared to more than five hundred witnesses who saw him face-to-face.

About two thousand years later, he also appeared to me—three times—because of my ignorance of who he was and is. He did not appear to me because I am more special than anyone else, because I am not. Quite the contrary, in fact. It takes more faith to believe without seeing.

Jesus' disciple Thomas said he would not believe in his Master's resurrection unless he saw the nail prints in his hands and the scar in his side. When Jesus appeared to him personally, he let Thomas touch the imprints from the nails and the sword. Then he said, "Thomas, because you have seen Me, you have believed. Blessed are those who have not seen and yet have believed" (John 20:29).

FOR MY FELLOW JEWS

I encourage my Jewish brothers and sisters around the world to search the Hebrew Scriptures, starting with the ones I have mentioned in this book. I am confident you will see that Jesus fulfilled all the prophecies concerning the coming of the Messiah.

You see, the foundation of what is now known as Christianity was birthed in Jerusalem amongst the Jewish people. The Old and New Testaments were written by Jews, and the first disciples of Jesus were all Jews.

I had no idea how Jewish the New Testament was in context, culture, and writing style. For example, I always thought Jesus' surname was Christ because his parents were "Joseph and Mary Christ." But I've learned that Christ is the Greek word for Messiah, or "anointed one." And Jesus is the English translation for his original Hebrew name, Yeshua, which means "salvation."

Jesus came for the whole world, but he came first to his own people. Now is the time for all Jews to recognize him for who he really is—not just a good man, not just a prophet, but the Messiah himself, as foretold by the ancient Hebrew prophecies.

A common misconception among Jews is that if they accept Jesus, they will no longer be Jews, that they will lose their Jewish identity and heritage. That was my initial fear when I accepted Jesus. But I quickly found out that it was groundless. In fact, the opposite happened. My Jewish identity was strengthened. I feel more connected now to the God of Abraham, the land of Israel, and my people than ever. I have come back to the God of my fathers by accepting the Messiah he sent. I am now a fulfilled Jew.

The core truth of the Bible, both Old and New Testaments, is that everyone has sinned, both Jews and Gentiles. But Jesus laid down his life to forgive us of all our sins. He did that for me, and he did it for you too. And he wants to show you the great plan he has for your life, which will exceed all your wildest dreams and expectations.

FOR THOSE WHO WANT A PERSONAL RELATIONSHIP WITH GOD THROUGH THE MESSIAH

If you have never accepted Jesus into your life, I encourage you to pray this simple prayer of faith:

> *Yeshua, I believe you are the Messiah, the promised one of Israel. Forgive me of my sins, and come live in my heart. I believe you died for me and rose from the dead after three days. I receive you as my Lord and my Savior. Amen.*

If you prayed that simple prayer, whether you are Jewish or Gentile, I'd love for you to let me know at cohen.geoffrey63@gmail.com. I would love to encourage you in your walk. Since you may feel isolated after praying to receive Yeshua, I can direct you to like-minded believers in your area and connect you to a local messianic congregation or church if you desire.

If you just accepted Jesus as your Messiah, you have made the best and most important decision of your life. Your adventure of a lifetime has just begun!

FOR ALL READERS

Walking with Jesus is a lifelong calling and a joyful journey. God knows we are frail and will make mistakes. But he wants us to live a life free from guilt and condemnation, because whoever the Son sets free is free indeed (John 8:36). His grace is more than sufficient to see us through every trial and tribulation life can throw at us, right to the very end. He who called you is faithful. He promised that he will never leave us or forsake us (Hebrews 13:5).

At the end of his earthly life, Jesus left the disciples with these comforting words: "Lo, I am with you always, even to the end of the age" (Matthew 28:20). This message applies to us today too. Jesus sacrificed his life to give you a full and abundant life. So relax and enjoy the journey!

Photo Album

Geoff at 17 with his Labrador Merlin

Geoff doing his speech at Barmitzvah reception to guests

Barmitsvah photo

Geoff with his parents, Ronald and Zena Cohen

Geoff with family at Barmitzvah, From right to left, his sister Barbara, Mother Zena, sister Trace, grandmother Fruma from Lithuania, his dad Ronnie, Grandfather Leslie from Lithuania, Aunt Rosalind and her husband.

Geoff in army uniform 1982

About the Author

Geoffrey Cohen is a South African-born Messianic Jew descended from the priestly tribe of Levi. After a dramatic and life-changing encounter with the God of Israel in 1984, Geoffrey took up a call to specialize in cross cultural ministry around the world with a specific focus on helping Jewish people come to a personal knowledge of their Messiah.

Geoffrey has ministered in many nations for decades, speaking in conferences, synagogues, Bible Schools, churches, and on radio and television. Geoffrey co-hosted a television show, Shalom Jerusalem, in Virginia. He has also appeared on The 700 Club, It's Supernatural (with Sid Roth), Daystar television network, and broadcasts throughout South America and regions of Africa. Geoffrey travels around the U.S. and the world with his wife, Tatiana, encouraging the Body of Messiah to love the God of Israel and reaching His Chosen people with the good news of their Messiah.

For more information, email Geoffrey at
cohen.geoffrey63@gmail.com or visit geoffreycohen.com.